Farm to Chef

Lynn Crawford

Farm to Chef

Cooking Through the Seasons

PENGUIN

an imprint of Penguin Canada, a division of Penguin Random House Canada Limited

Canada • USA • UK • Ireland • Australia • New Zealand • India • South Africa • China

First published 2017

www.penguinrandomhouse.ca

LIBRARY AND ARCHIVES CANADA CATALOGUING IN PUBLICATION

Crawford, Lynn, author
    Farm to chef : cooking through the seasons / Lynn Crawford.

ISBN 978-0-14-319360-9 (hardcover)
ISBN 978-0-14-319361-6 (electronic)

    1. Seasonal cooking. 2. Cookbooks. I. Title.

TX714.C737 2017   641.5'64   C2016-907476-5

Book design by CS Richardson
Food photography by Virginia Macdonald

Printed and bound in China

10 9 8 7 6 5 4 3 2 1

Penguin
Random House
PENGUIN CANADA

This cookbook is for my beautiful family, Lora and Addie Pepper

Also by Lynn Crawford

At Home with Lynn Crawford

Lynn Crawford's Pitchin' In

CONTENTS

INTRODUCTION

To cook . . . there is nothing else I'd rather do. Consider this book your official invitation to cook with me for an entire year, to discover all the seasons together. I am, as you may already know, a champion of all things local and seasonal. Supporting local farmers and growers has become my way of life both at home and in my restaurants. I have such admiration for those who have dedicated their lives to growing, harvesting and sharing ingredients bursting with flavour and perfection.

Every season is memorable for its own special reasons. Spring is about beginnings, a season when you are completely re-energized. The weeks of grey and cold are over, that final layer of snow melts away, and we finally come out of hibernation. I find the first signs of spring so uplifting: the warmth of the sun in the morning, that fresh crisp air, a robin's nest that sits on the ledge just outside my bedroom window with tiny blue eggs nestled in it. Everything is alive again. It's time to start planting, planning and mapping out the firsts of the season. I get excited about heading back to the farmers' market, where everyone feels a genuine warmth and excitement about the season ahead. Farmers unveil the bundles of asparagus, bushels of ramps and fiddleheads, baskets of strawberries, and rhubarb for days. We're reacquainted with the familiar faces that we haven't seen in months. It is a short season, and there is not an exuberant amount of ingredients to work with, but what there is has so much personality, vibrancy, intensity and beauty.

Summer is about sharing. It's time to explore, spend time outdoors, cook with family and friends, go on a road trip and barbecue. For me it is about gathering around the campfire, the laughter, the stories we share. I love the fun and lightheartedness that summer brings, and the food for me must always reflect that. There is a certain beauty and simplicity when cooking at this time of year. You will never run out of fresh, flavourful ingredients: those brilliant cherries and beans, sweet and tender corn dripping with butter, grilled summer squash, tomatoes just picked from the vine seasoned with nothing more than chilies and basil, and of course a refreshing cocktail or two. Letting the food speak for itself is the best thing about cooking in summer.

I love everything about the autumn: drives up to the cottage, warm sweaters, the gold and red hues of the fall leaves, fields of pumpkins, the stillness of the lake, getting a roaring fire going, the smell of warm spices. In the kitchen, autumn is all about the harvest. I love baking, roasting and preserving. It's the season to take advantage of the last big harvest before winter. Bring out the big pots for soups and stews and the jars for jams and jellies, and gather the apples, beets or grapes. The Sunday roast dinner is back, and there is always a mug of warm apple cider and a plate of crisp pear fritters nearby.

When I think of winter, I think about family, friends and comfort. It's a wonderful opportunity to be at home with the ones you love. When winter hits, I'm ready for it. I get excited about the first snowstorm, and even more so, the cellar I've stocked with everything that has been preserved. Winter and eating go hand in hand. Bring on the baking—breads, cookies, loaves— and savoury rich sauces! Surround yourself with the comfort of potatoes, onions, squashes and hearty roots like rutabaga and turnips. I embrace the season and relish (no pun intended) all it has to offer. I love to invite friends over for a spontaneous potluck after an afternoon of skating. It's a magical time of year.

I can't wait for you to discover and be inspired by the fruits and vegetables local to your towns and cities. This collection of recipes should provide an encouraging foundation for any home cook's seasonal journey. Not only were these recipes so much fun to create, but they are an absolute pleasure to prepare, and most important, they are simply delicious. I guarantee many will become your go-to favourites. Cooking really is all about sharing, and I'm thrilled to share with you dishes that celebrate and embrace the beauty and abundance of the seasons.

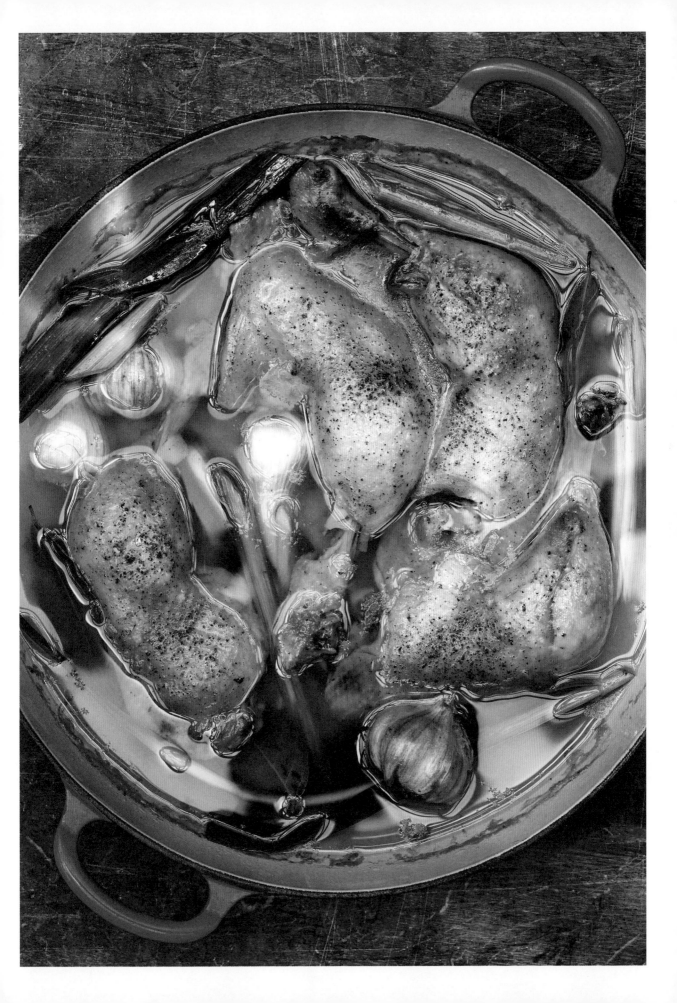

Fall

APPLES

One of my favourite sights at the farmers' market in the early fall is bushel upon bushel of all the gorgeous apple varieties on display—Cortlands, Empires, Idareds, Spartans and McIntosh, just to name a few. I have great child-hood memories of fun-filled afternoons spent picking apples in the orchards near Meaford and Thornbury, in Ontario. So many dishes were made with all those apples that came home with us! One of our regular family dinners was a classic no-fuss pan-fried pork chop with just salt, pepper and a little butter with apples. It is still one of my favourite comfort meals. I've updated the dish slightly for my Pork Chop with Apple-Braised Cabbage. I also couldn't leave out a really great apple pie recipe, could I? It's the perfect way to finish off any meal, especially with a mug of Hot Buttered Bourbon Cider.

When the leaves are falling and there's a bit of chill in the air, everyone deserves a comforting treat. I highly suggest putting a pot on the stove and making this recipe. What is more satisfying than the smell of simmering apple cider with cinnamon and ginger? Combine that with the taste of hot buttered bourbon, and there is nothing better!

HOT BUTTERED BOURBON CIDER

1. In a large saucepan, combine cider, brown sugar, cinnamon and ginger. Simmer for 10 minutes, then remove from heat and steep for 15 minutes.

2. Whisk in butter, bourbon, lemon juice and nutmeg. Strain into a measuring cup. Pour cider into glass mugs and serve garnished with apple slices.

Serves 4

3 cups (750 mL) pressed sweet apple cider
2 tablespoons (30 mL) dark brown sugar
1 cinnamon stick
2 thin slices peeled fresh ginger
3 tablespoons (45 mL) unsalted butter
4 ounces (125 mL) bourbon
2 tablespoons (30 mL) lemon juice
Pinch of nutmeg
Thinly sliced red apple, for garnish

Mostarda is a condiment made of candied fruit and preserved with mustard seeds, very similar to a chutney. I love serving this mostarda with my Pork Chops with Apple-Braised Cabbage (page 8). The classic combination of fruit and mustard makes the pork shine.

APPLE MOSTARDA

1. In a medium saucepan over medium heat, melt butter. Add apples and cook until softened, about 5 minutes, stirring often. Stir in sugar and shallots and cook until sugar melts, about 2 minutes. Add brandy and cook until alcohol evaporates, about 1 minute. Add vinegar, raisins, ginger and orange and lemon peels. Stir to combine, bring mixture to a boil, then reduce heat to low and simmer, stirring occasionally, until mixture thickens, about 15 minutes.

2. Stir in Dijon and whole-grain mustards and cook for 5 minutes more. Season to taste with salt and pepper. Discard orange and lemon peels, if desired.

3. Spoon mostarda into an airtight container and refrigerate until ready to use. Keep refrigerated for up to 2 weeks. For optimal flavour, let mostarda rest at room temperature for 30 minutes before serving.

Makes about 1 cup (250 mL)

3 tablespoons (45 mL) unsalted butter
2 apples, such as Pink Lady or Gala, peeled, cored and diced
¼ cup (60 mL) dark brown sugar
1 shallot, minced
2 tablespoons (30 mL) brandy
¼ cup (60 mL) apple cider vinegar
¼ cup (60 mL) seedless golden raisins
1 tablespoon (15 mL) grated peeled fresh ginger
2 strips orange peel
2 strips lemon peel
1 tablespoon (15 mL) Dijon mustard
1 tablespoon (15 mL) whole-grain mustard
Kosher salt and cracked black pepper

This tasty "butter" doesn't actually have any dairy in it. It is pure apple, puréed with lots of warm spices and peppercorns. Making apple butter is a wonderful way to preserve this staple of the autumn harvest. It is incredible on a slice of buttered toast or on pork, like my Pork Chops with Apple-Braised Cabbage (page 8).

SPICED APPLE BUTTER

1. Preheat oven to 425°F (220°C) and line a baking sheet with parchment paper.

2. Place apples cut side up on the baking sheet. Sprinkle with star anise, cinnamon, cloves, mustard seeds, peppercorns, coriander seeds, red pepper flakes and salt, and drizzle with oil. Bake apples until they are fork-tender, about 30 minutes.

3. Remove cinnamon sticks and star anise, then place apples in a blender and process until smooth, adding a little water, if necessary. Refrigerate in an airtight container for up to a week.

Makes about 2 cups (500 mL)

6 large baking apples, such as Gravenstein or Honeycrisp, halved lengthwise
4 small star anise, broken into pieces
2 small cinnamon sticks, broken in half
1 teaspoon (5 mL) whole cloves
1 teaspoon (5 mL) yellow mustard seeds
1 teaspoon (5 mL) pink peppercorns
1 teaspoon (5 mL) black peppercorns
1 teaspoon (5 mL) coriander seeds
½ teaspoon (2 mL) red pepper flakes
½ teaspoon (2 mL) kosher salt
2 tablespoons (30 mL) vegetable oil

Pork and cabbage is a classic combination, and so is pork and apples. When all three ingredients come together, get ready for a hearty meal that is made for autumn. This is the perfect supper to follow an afternoon of apple picking.

PORK CHOPS with APPLE-BRAISED CABBAGE

Serves 4

2 tablespoons (30 mL) canola oil
1 small yellow onion, halved and
thinly sliced
1 tablespoon (15 mL) dark brown
sugar
½ cup (125 mL) dry red wine
5 cups (1.25 L) cored and thinly sliced
red cabbage
Kosher salt and cracked black pepper
2 Gala apples, halved lengthwise,
cored and thinly sliced
¼ cup (60 mL) Spiced Apple Butter
(page 5)
2 tablespoons (30 mL) chopped
flat-leaf parsley
2 tablespoons (30 mL) olive oil
4 bone-in centre-cut pork chops
(about 8 ounces/225 g each)
¼ cup (60 mL) Apple Mostarda
(page 5)
Herbs or seedlings, for garnish,
if desired

1. In a large skillet over medium heat, heat canola oil. Add onion and cook until translucent, about 3 minutes. Add sugar and wine and cook, stirring often, until mixture is syrupy, about 10 minutes. Stir in cabbage and season to taste with salt and pepper. Simmer until cabbage is tender, about 10 minutes more. Add apple slices and cook until softened, about 10 minutes, stirring often. Stir in apple butter and parsley. Remove from heat and keep warm.

2. In another skillet over medium heat, heat olive oil. Season pork chops well with salt and pepper. Add to skillet and cook until golden brown and cooked through, about 5 minutes per side.

3. To serve, spoon cabbage onto each plate. Place a pork chop over cabbage, top with mostarda and garnish with herbs or seedlings, if using.

I love pie. A good apple pie stuffed with just-picked apples tossed with cinnamon, nutmeg and sugar nestled in a buttery crust . . . oh yes, that's what I'm talking about. But which apple to choose, you ask? Tart or sweet, or a combination of both—I will leave that decision up to you.

HARVEST APPLE PIE

Make the Pie Dough

1. In a food processor, combine flour, sugar, salt, butter and shortening. Pulse until mixture resembles pea-size crumbles. Add 6 tablespoons (90 mL) water and continue to pulse until dough comes together. Squeeze a small amount of dough between your fingers, and if it is very crumbly, add more water, 1 tablespoon (15 mL) at a time. Do not over-process. Divide dough in half and flatten each half into a disc. Wrap discs in plastic wrap and chill for at least 1 hour before using.

2. Preheat oven to 400°F (200°C).

3. On a lightly floured work surface, roll out each disc of dough into a 12-inch (30 cm) circle. Fold one round into quarters and place dough into an ungreased 9-inch (23 cm) pie plate. Unfold dough, then press firmly against bottom and sides. Trim crust to ½ inch (1 cm) over edge of pie plate. Set aside.

Make the Apple Filling and Bake the Pie

4. In a large bowl, combine melted butter, granulated and brown sugars, cinnamon and nutmeg. Add apples and lemon juice and toss lightly to coat. Dust apples with flour and toss again. Spoon apple mixture into prepared crust.

5. Brush edge of bottom crust with some egg wash. Top with the second pastry round and trim edges to about 1 inch (2.5 cm) over the rim. Tuck edge of the top crust under edge of the bottom crust and crimp both together with your fingers or a fork. Brush entire top crust with egg wash, then sprinkle with 1 tablespoon (15 mL) sugar. Cut three 1-inch (2.5 cm) slits in top crust. Bake until crust is golden brown and filling is bubbling, about 1 hour. Let cool completely before serving.

Makes 1 pie

Pie Dough

3 cups (750 mL) all-purpose flour, plus more for dusting

2 tablespoons (30 mL) granulated sugar, plus 1 tablespoon (15 mL) for sprinkling on top

1 teaspoon (5 mL) salt

¾ cup (175 mL) cold unsalted butter, cut into chunks

⅓ cup (75 mL) cold vegetable shortening, cut into chunks

6 to 8 tablespoons (90 to 125 mL) cold water

1 large egg, lightly beaten with 1 tablespoon (15 mL) water, for egg wash

Apple Filling

2 tablespoons (30 mL) unsalted butter, melted

¼ cup (60 mL) granulated sugar

¼ cup (60 mL) firmly packed brown sugar

1 teaspoon (5 mL) cinnamon

½ teaspoon (2 mL) nutmeg

8 tart apples, such as Granny Smith, peeled, cored and thinly sliced

2 tablespoons (30 mL) lemon juice

¼ cup (60 mL) all-purpose flour

BEETS

Beets! Is there another vegetable that more people have mixed feelings about? (Brussels sprouts, maybe, but we'll get to them later.) Personally, I love beets—their earthy, sweet flavour, their shocking deep, rich red colour, their tender texture and their old-fashioned good-for-you-ness. Beets are available all year round but are at their best in late summer and autumn. Look for firm, rounded beets with smooth skins and leafy greens that look alive, a good indication that the beets are super-fresh. These nutritious leaves can be prepared just as you would spinach. I've got some new and fun ways to try this wonderful vegetable: in a delicious Raw and Pickled Beet Salad with Plums, Dill Sour Cream and Pistachios; and dressed up for company in my Arctic Char with Beet and Horseradish Relish.

Arctic char is a great sustainable choice if you like salmon or trout. Its delicate texture and clean, mild flavour pair beautifully with the horseradish kick of the fresh and herby beet relish. The keys to preparing this fish are to allow it to come to room temperature before frying so it cooks evenly, and also to season it really well before frying. Lastly, make sure the skin is nice and crispy before removing the fish from the pan. You won't regret this last step when you bite into the delicious, crackling exterior.

ARCTIC CHAR with BEET and HORSERADISH RELISH

1. In a medium bowl, gently fold together beets, celery, celery leaves, chives, horseradish and olive oil until combined. Season to taste with salt and pepper.

2. In a large skillet over medium-high heat, heat canola oil. Season fish well on both sides with salt and pepper. Add fish to pan skin side down and fry until crisp and golden, about 2 minutes per side.

3. To serve, divide beet mixture between plates and top with char skin side up. Garnish with sea salt and microgreens and serve immediately.

Serves 2

1 cup (250 mL) My Dad's Pickled Beets (page 15) or store-bought sliced pickled beets
¼ cup (60 mL) thinly sliced celery
1 tablespoon (15 mL) coarsely chopped celery leaves
1 tablespoon (15 mL) finely chopped chives
1 tablespoon (15 mL) freshly grated horseradish
1 tablespoon (15 mL) extra-virgin olive oil
Kosher salt and cracked black pepper
1 tablespoon (15 mL) canola oil
2 skin-on Arctic char fillets (about 5 ounces/140 g each), patted dry
Maldon sea salt and microgreens, for garnish

Pickled beets are just marvellous. Preparing them brings back so many memories of my father. Every year he pickled beets, filling the kitchen counters with mismatched jars all ready to be filled. I distinctly remember the smell of vinegar, the sounds of our laughter and our bright purple hands. He loved beets . . . and so do I.

MY DAD'S PICKLED BEETS

1. Tie star anise, cinnamon, red pepper flakes, mustard seeds, peppercorns and cloves in a square of cheesecloth, creating a spice bag.

2. In a stockpot, combine beets, sugar, vinegar, wine, salt and spice bag. Add enough water to cover the beets. Bring to a boil over high heat, then reduce heat to medium-low and simmer until beets are fork-tender. Depending on their size, this will take anywhere from 45 to 90 minutes.

3. While beets are cooking, sterilize the jars and lids. Place 6 clean 1-pint (500 mL) mason jars on a rack in a boiling water canner. Add 6 sealing discs (but not screw bands). Cover jars with water and simmer for about 5 minutes at 180°F (82°C). Keep jars and sealing discs in the water until ready to use.

4. Drain beets, reserving the cooking liquid. Discard spice bag. Rinse beets under cold water. Wearing latex gloves, peel skins from beets. Slice beets into rounds.

5. Fill sterilized jars with beets, leaving 1-inch (2.5 cm) headspace. Add pickling liquid to cover beets, leaving ½-inch (1 cm) headspace. Wipe jar rims clean if necessary. Centre a hot sealing disc on a jar rim and twist on a screw band just until fingertip tight.

6. Return filled jars to rack in canner. Cover pot and process jars at a full boil for 30 minutes. Remove jars and place them upright on a protected counter. Cool upright, undisturbed, for 24 hours.

7. After cooling, check jar seals. Sealed discs should curve downward and do not move when pressed. Label jars and store in a cool, dark place. For best quality, use within 1 year.

Makes about six 1-pint (500 mL) jars

2 whole star anise
1 cinnamon stick
1 teaspoon (5 mL) red pepper flakes
1 teaspoon (5 mL) yellow mustard seeds
1 teaspoon (5 mL) pink peppercorns
1 teaspoon (5 mL) black peppercorns
½ teaspoon (2 mL) whole cloves
4 pounds (1.8 kg) red beets, trimmed and scrubbed clean
2 cups (500 mL) granulated sugar
2 cups (500 mL) red wine vinegar
2 cups (500 mL) dry red wine
¼ cup (60 mL) kosher salt

Borscht may be served hot or cold, chunky or strained, creamed with dairy or without. The base of the soup is beets and an acid, usually vinegar, lemon juice or cultured beet juice. Each country has its own variation of this iconic soup—actually, each cook in each town will have their own version. For this special recipe, I called upon Lora's Babka Olga, who at 92 still makes her borscht for family gatherings

BABKA'S BORSCHT

Serves 8

2 tablespoons (30 mL) extra-virgin olive oil
1 cup (250 mL) diced yellow onion
3 cloves garlic, minced
1 teaspoon (5 mL) caraway seeds
4 cups (1 L) coarsely grated peeled beets
3 cups (750 mL) finely shredded red cabbage
2 cups (500 mL) coarsely grated peeled carrots
6 cups (1.5 L) vegetable stock
1 can (19 ounces/540 mL) tomato juice
2 tablespoons (30 mL) apple cider vinegar
1 tablespoon (15 mL) dark brown sugar
1 sprig thyme
2 bay leaves
Kosher salt and cracked black pepper
Sour cream and microgreens, for garnish, if desired

1. In a Dutch oven over medium heat, heat oil. Add onion, garlic and caraway seeds and cook until onion is translucent, about 5 minutes, stirring often.

2. Add beets, cabbage, carrots, stock, tomato juice, vinegar, sugar, thyme and bay leaves. Bring to a boil, then reduce heat to medium-low and simmer until vegetables are tender, 30 to 40 minutes. Discard bay leaves. Season well with salt and pepper.

3. Ladle borscht into warm soup bowls, garnish with sour cream and microgreens, if using, and serve immediately.

This recipe uses both pickled and raw beets. That earthy sweetness of the raw beets is delicious paired with the sharper flavours of the mustard and the creamy dill sour cream. I love how the bite of the pickled beets contrasts so nicely with the sweet ripe plums.

RAW and PICKLED BEET SALAD with PLUMS, DILL SOUR CREAM and PISTACHIOS

Serves 4

Brown Derby Vinaigrette
Makes about 1 cup (250 mL)
¼ cup (60 mL) red wine vinegar
1 tablespoon (15 mL) balsamic vinegar
1 tablespoon (15 mL) Dijon mustard
1 tablespoon (15 mL) honey
2 teaspoons (10 mL) Worcestershire sauce
¼ teaspoon (1 mL) salt
Juice of ½ lemon
⅔ cup (150 mL) canola oil

Dill Sour Cream
½ cup (125 mL) sour cream
1 tablespoon (15 mL) finely chopped dill
1 tablespoon (15 mL) whole-grain mustard (I like Kozlik's Triple Crunch Mustard)
1 teaspoon (5 mL) Dijon mustard
1 teaspoon (5 mL) kosher salt
¼ teaspoon (1 mL) cracked black pepper

Beet Salad
2 cups (500 mL) torn beet greens
1 cup My Dad's Pickled Beets (page 15) or store-bought sliced pickled beets
1 candy cane beet, thinly sliced into rounds
1 plum, sliced into thin wedges
2 tablespoons (30 mL) coarsely chopped pistachios

Make the Brown Derby Vinaigrette
1. Whisk together red wine and balsamic vinegars, mustard, honey, Worcestershire sauce, salt and lemon juice until well combined. Slowly whisk in oil until emulsified. Cover and refrigerate until ready to use.

Make the Dill Sour Cream
2. In a small bowl, whisk together sour cream, dill, whole-grain and Dijon mustards, salt and pepper until combined.

Prepare the Beet Salad
3. In a medium bowl, toss beet greens with 1 tablespoon (15 mL) Brown Derby Vinaigrette.

4. To serve, spoon Dill Sour Cream onto a serving plate. Arrange greens, pickled beets, candy cane beets and plum wedges on top. Sprinkle with pistachios and serve immediately.

BROCCOLI

Sometimes it's not about reinventing the wheel—it's about enjoying what we love about tried-and-true staples. That's how I feel about our good friend broccoli. It's a dependable, staple green in my home, a solid sidekick to whatever protein or grain you want to pair it with. Broccoli's sturdy nature means it can take a little heat—literally. A simple, straight-forward charring in a hot cast-iron pan brings out an unexpected sweetness, and you'll love the flavours in my Broccoli with Chili, Garlic and Shallots—that combination is completely addictive. Let's talk about the ideal Broccoli and Cheese Sauce too. Bright green, lovingly cooked florets bathed in a dreamy creamy zingy sauce—it really doesn't get more delicious than that.

Everyone likes to make the classic holiday broccoli cheese bake, which unfortunately usually ends up as an overbaked mess. My version is an easier way to enjoy this classic, without overcooking the broccoli. The cheese sauce is easily adaptable—swap in your favourite cheese (or cheeses!).

BROCCOLI and CHEESE SAUCE

1. In a small saucepan over medium heat, melt butter. Whisk in flour and cook, whisking, for 1 minute. Gradually whisk in milk and cook, whisking constantly, until thickened, about 7 minutes. Remove from heat and stir in cheddar, mustard and nutmeg until blended. Season to taste with salt and pepper. Keep sauce warm over very low heat until broccoli is cooked.

2. In a saucepan of boiling salted water, blanch broccoli for 4 minutes. Drain broccoli in a colander, shaking gently to remove excess water.

3. Transfer broccoli to a serving bowl and spoon warm cheese sauce over top. Serve immediately.

Serves 4

2 tablespoons (30 mL) unsalted butter
2 tablespoons (30 mL) all-purpose flour
1 cup (250 mL) milk
1 cup (250 mL) grated extra-old cheddar cheese
1 tablespoon (15 mL) Dijon mustard (I like Kozlik's Amazing Maple Mustard)
Pinch of freshly grated nutmeg
Kosher salt and cracked black pepper
4 cups (1 L) broccoli florets

I like to think that eating fried vegetables is a healthy sin, and I love that you can tempura-fry any kind of vegetable. This is an excellent recipe to pull out when friends are over. Packed with the bold flavours of ginger, lemongrass and chilies, it's a real crowd-pleaser!

TEMPURA BROCCOLI with COCONUT PEANUT SAUCE

Make the Coconut Peanut Sauce

1. In a medium saucepan over medium heat, heat oil. Add ginger, shallot, lemongrass and chili and cook for 2 minutes, stirring constantly. Add coconut milk, peanut butter, soy sauce, sambal oelek and lime zest and juice; whisk to combine. Cook sauce until thoroughly heated, then transfer to a bowl and cool to room temperature.

Prepare the Tempura Broccoli

2. In a deep, narrow bowl, whisk together flour, cornstarch and enough sparkling water to achieve a consistency like crêpe batter.

3. In a deep medium saucepan, heat 4 inches (10 cm) of oil to 375°F (190°C).

4. Working in batches, dip broccoli spears one at a time into batter, then carefully place in hot oil and fry until crisp and golden, about 3 minutes. With a slotted spoon, transfer broccoli to paper towel to drain and season lightly with salt and pepper. Repeat with remaining broccoli spears.

5. Garnish tempura broccoli with peanuts, cilantro and chili, and serve immediately with Coconut Peanut Sauce.

Serves 4

Coconut Peanut Sauce

1 tablespoon (15 mL) canola oil
2 tablespoons (30 mL) minced peeled fresh ginger
1 tablespoon (15 mL) minced shallot
1 tablespoon (15 mL) minced lemongrass
1 tablespoon (15 mL) minced Fresno chili
1 can (14 ounces/400 mL) coconut milk
½ cup (125 mL) peanut butter
2 tablespoons (30 mL) soy sauce
1 tablespoon (15 mL) sambal oelek
Zest and juice of 1 lime

Tempura Broccoli

½ cup (125 mL) all-purpose flour
2 tablespoons (30 mL) cornstarch
1 to 1⅓ cups (250 to 325 mL) sparkling water
Vegetable oil, for deep-frying
1 head broccoli, florets cut into spears
Kosher salt and cracked black pepper

To Serve

1 tablespoon (15 mL) chopped roasted peanuts
1 tablespoon (15 mL) finely chopped cilantro
1 teaspoon (5 mL) minced Fresno chili

I simply love the nutty, roasted broccoli coated with chilies, garlic and shallots. This recipe will make a broccoli lover out of anyone.

BROCCOLI with CHILI, GARLIC and SHALLOTS

Serves 4

1 bunch broccoli, cut into florets
4 tablespoons (60 mL) olive oil,
    divided
2 shallots, finely chopped
2 cloves garlic, minced
1 tablespoon (15 mL) finely chopped
    Fresno chili
2 tablespoons (30 mL) unsalted butter
2 tablespoons (30 mL) lemon juice
Kosher salt and cracked black pepper

1. In a saucepan of boiling salted water, blanch broccoli for 2 minutes. With a slotted spoon, transfer to a bowl of ice water to stop the cooking process. Drain florets and pat dry with paper towel.

2. In a large skillet over medium heat, heat 2 tablespoons (30 mL) oil. Working in batches if necessary so as not to crowd the pan, sear florets until slightly charred, about 3 minutes per side. Place cooked florets in a bowl.

3. Add remaining 2 tablespoons (30 mL) oil to the skillet, along with shallots, garlic, chili and butter. Cook until shallots are translucent, about 5 minutes, stirring often. Add reserved florets to the skillet, add lemon juice and toss to coat. Season to taste with salt and pepper and serve immediately.

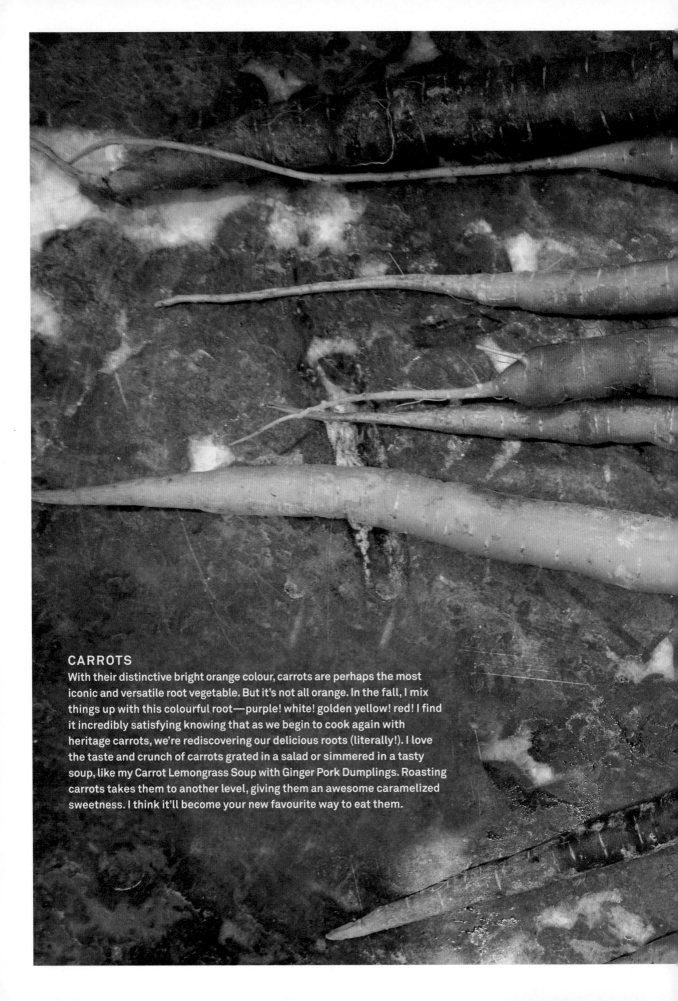

CARROTS

With their distinctive bright orange colour, carrots are perhaps the most iconic and versatile root vegetable. But it's not all orange. In the fall, I mix things up with this colourful root—purple! white! golden yellow! red! I find it incredibly satisfying knowing that as we begin to cook again with heritage carrots, we're rediscovering our delicious roots (literally!). I love the taste and crunch of carrots grated in a salad or simmered in a tasty soup, like my Carrot Lemongrass Soup with Ginger Pork Dumplings. Roasting carrots takes them to another level, giving them an awesome caramelized sweetness. I think it'll become your new favourite way to eat them.

This simple side dish is carrots from top to bottom. Roasted grapes bring out the natural sweetness of the caramelized carrots, and the creamy, rich carrot-top dressing completes the dish. Carrot tops are loaded with vitamins and give the dressing an herbaceous, almost carrot-like flavour I think you'll love!

PAN-ROASTED CARROTS with SALT-ROASTED GRAPES and CARROT-TOP GREEN GODDESS DRESSING

Serves 4

Carrot-Top Green Goddess Dressing
1 ripe avocado, peeled and pitted
1 cup (250 mL) mayonnaise
½ cup (125 mL) sour cream
1 shallot, chopped
1 clove garlic, peeled
½ cup (125 mL) loosely packed
    carrot-top greens
2 tablespoons (30 mL) chopped chives
2 tablespoons (30 mL) lemon juice
Kosher salt and cracked black pepper

Pan-Roasted Carrots
1 tablespoon (15 mL) canola oil
1 tablespoon (15 mL) unsalted butter
1 clove garlic, peeled
2 teaspoons (10 mL) dark brown sugar
Juice of 1 orange
1 sprig thyme
1 bunch rainbow carrots (about
    1 pound/450 g), peeled

Salt-Roasted Grapes
1½ cups (375 mL) mixed seedless
    grapes, halved lengthwise
1 tablespoon (15 mL) grapeseed oil
1 teaspoon (5 mL) kosher salt

To Serve
2 tablespoons (30 mL) toasted
    slivered almonds
Coarsely chopped dill fronds

1. Preheat oven to 425°F (220°C) and line a baking sheet with parchment paper.

Make the Carrot-Top Green Goddess Dressing
2. Place avocado, mayonnaise, sour cream, shallot, garlic, carrot-top greens, chives and lemon juice in a blender and process until blended. Season to taste with salt and pepper. Transfer to a bowl, cover and refrigerate until ready to use.

Prepare the Pan-Roasted Carrots
3. In a skillet over medium heat, heat canola oil and butter until shimmering. With the back of your knife, crush the garlic clove and add to the pan. Stir in sugar and orange juice. Add thyme and carrots and cook until golden and tender, about 15 minutes, turning frequently. Remove from heat and discard thyme.

Prepare the Salt-Roasted Grapes
4. Meanwhile, toss grapes with grapeseed oil and salt and spread on the baking sheet. Roast grapes in oven until slightly wilted, about 5 minutes.

Assemble the Salad
5. Spread ½ cup (125 mL) Carrot-Top Green Goddess Dressing in centre of a serving platter and arrange carrots on top. Spoon grapes over carrots, and garnish with almonds and dill. Serve immediately.

This soup seriously delivers. Along with the sweet, earthy carrots, it is jazzed up with ginger, lemongrass, garlic, red chili and coconut milk, flavours that match beautifully. This aromatic dish is finished off with pork dumplings, which happen to be my kryptonite. I think they'll become yours, too, so I suggest making lots. They freeze well.

CARROT LEMONGRASS SOUP with GINGER PORK DUMPLINGS

Prepare the Ginger Pork Dumplings

1. In a medium bowl, mix the pork, soy sauce, chives, cilantro, ginger, chili, salt and pepper together until combined.

2. Working with 1 wonton wrapper at a time, spoon 1 teaspoon (5 mL) pork mixture into centre of wrapper and brush edges lightly with some egg. Bring up corners to meet in centre, gently pushing out any air pockets; pinch edges to seal. Refrigerate until needed.

Make the Carrot Lemongrass Soup

3. In a large pot over medium heat, melt butter. Stir in oil, onion, garlic, lemongrass, chili and ginger. Cook until onions soften, about 10 minutes. Add orange zest and juice, carrots, stock and coconut milk. Cover and cook until carrots are very tender, about 25 minutes.

4. Working in batches, transfer soup to a blender and purée. Return soup to pot and heat thoroughly. Season to taste with salt and pepper.

Cook the Ginger Pork Dumplings

5. A few minutes before the soup is ready to serve, bring a pot of water to a gentle boil. Add dumplings in batches and boil until cooked in the middle, about 5 minutes.

6. To serve, ladle soup into 4 warmed bowls. Place Ginger Pork Dumplings on top, garnish with chives and serve immediately.

Serves 6

Ginger Pork Dumplings
½ pound (225 g) lean ground pork
1 tablespoon (15 mL) soy sauce
1 tablespoon (15 mL) finely chopped chives
1 tablespoon (15 mL) finely chopped cilantro
1 teaspoon (5 mL) minced peeled fresh ginger
1 teaspoon (5 mL) minced serrano chili
Pinch of kosher salt and cracked black pepper
24 wonton wrappers
1 large egg, lightly beaten

Carrot Lemongrass Soup
2 tablespoons (30 mL) unsalted butter
1 tablespoon (15 mL) extra-virgin olive oil
¼ cup (60 mL) diced yellow onion
1 clove garlic, minced
1 tablespoon (15 mL) minced lemongrass
1 tablespoon (15 mL) minced serrano chili
2 teaspoons (10 mL) chopped peeled fresh ginger
Zest and juice of 1 orange
4 cups (1 L) carrots, peeled and cut crosswise into ½-inch (1 cm) pieces
4 cups (1 L) chicken stock
1 can (14 ounces/400 mL) full-fat coconut milk
Kosher salt and cracked black pepper

To Serve
Finely chopped chives

CAULIFLOWER

Is it just me or is cauliflower a real comeback kid these days? We're all familiar with the snowy white florets, but new varieties are becoming popular too: chartreuse-coloured Romanesco, purple, green, yellow and even mini cauliflower are popping up everywhere. Perhaps its newfound popularity has to do with how versatile all the varieties are—roasted whole with punchy spices, puréed, stir-fried, served au gratin with béchamel sauce, in a casserole and soups, fried in a crispy tempura batter, the list goes on! I've shared recipes that show off cauliflower's diverse personality, including a few showstoppers: a stunning Cauliflower Romesco and a wonderfully rich Thyme and Garlic Butter Basted Beef Filets with Cauliflower Purée.

This dish reminds me of my time living in New York. I would go to my favourite Italian restaurant, Lupa, almost every Sunday, late afternoon, and order a glass of wine and the cauliflower pasta. This is my spin on those flavours of salty prosciutto, roasted cauliflower and rosemary. To make this meal even more decadent, serve the pasta alongside my Veal Saltimbocca with Sautéed Spinach (page 59).

CAULIFLOWER PASTA with PECORINO and ROSEMARY

Serves 2 to 4

4 tablespoons (60 mL) extra-virgin
    olive oil, divided
½ head cauliflower, cut into 1-inch
    (2.5 cm) florets (about 4 cups/1 L)
1 pound (450 g) spaccatelle or other
    short curved pasta
Vegetable oil
2 to 4 slices prosciutto, torn into large
    strips
2 shallots, thinly sliced into rings
1 tablespoon (15 mL) fresh rosemary
    leaves
2 teaspoons (10 mL) minced garlic
½ teaspoon (2 mL) cracked black
    pepper
2 tablespoons (30 mL) unsalted butter
Kosher salt and more cracked black
    pepper
½ cup (125 mL) grated pecorino
    cheese
2 tablespoons (30 mL) finely chopped
    chives

1. Preheat oven to 325°F (160°C).

2. In a skillet over medium heat, heat 2 tablespoons (30 mL) olive oil until shimmering. Working in batches, fry cauliflower until golden brown, about 10 minutes. Transfer to a baking sheet and keep warm in oven.

3. Meanwhile, cook pasta according to package directions until al dente. Drain. In a large bowl, toss with enough vegetable oil to coat well. Set aside.

4. Return skillet to medium heat and add remaining 2 tablespoons (30 mL) olive oil, prosciutto, shallots and rosemary. Cook until shallots are golden, about 5 minutes, stirring frequently. Add garlic, pepper and butter and cook 2 minutes more.

5. Add shallot mixture and reserved cauliflower to pasta and fold gently to combine. Season to taste with salt and pepper. Garnish with pecorino and chives and serve immediately.

This is a great recipe for Meatless Monday—or any day, for that matter. An entire head of cauliflower is roasted until gloriously browned. The caramelized, nutty cauliflower is then served with a rich smoky-sweet romesco sauce that has Spanish flair and a little heat. This is one sauce you have to keep in your fridge because it is wonderful on absolutely everything—vegetables, sandwiches, pasta, grilled fish, roast chicken . . . all love romesco.

CAULIFLOWER ROMESCO

1. Preheat oven to 350°F (180°C) and line a baking sheet with parchment paper.

2. Cut leaves from cauliflower and trim root end. Place cauliflower on baking sheet, drizzle with 3 tablespoons (45 mL) oil and sprinkle with rosemary. Bake until golden and tender, about 1 hour.

3. Meanwhile, in a large skillet over medium heat, heat 1 tablespoon (15 mL) oil. Add tomato, garlic, red onion and chili and cook until slightly charred on all sides. Add paprika and season to taste with salt and pepper. Continue cooking until liquid from the tomatoes has evaporated.

4. Transfer charred vegetables to a food processor. Add roasted peppers, almonds, bread cubes, vinegar and remaining 1 teaspoon (5 mL) oil. Process until combined and fairly smooth, adding more oil if necessary. Season to taste with salt and pepper.

5. Cut the baked cauliflower into quarters and spoon romesco sauce all over cauliflower. Sprinkle with Parmesan and continue baking until cheese melts, about 10 minutes more.

6. Transfer cauliflower to a serving dish and sprinkle with parsley.

Serves 6

1 head cauliflower
4 tablespoons (60 mL) plus 1 teaspoon
    (5 mL) extra-virgin olive oil, divided
1 teaspoon (5 mL) chopped rosemary
1 vine-ripened tomato, cut in half
    crosswise
2 cloves garlic, peeled and smashed
½ red onion, coarsely chopped
½ Fresno chili, coarsely chopped
1 teaspoon (5 mL) smoked paprika
Kosher salt and cracked black pepper
2 roasted red bell peppers, seeded
    and chopped
1 cup (250 mL) toasted sliced
    almonds
½ cup (125 mL) toasted bread cubes
2 tablespoons (30 mL) sherry vinegar
½ cup (125 mL) finely grated
    Parmesan cheese
2 tablespoons (30 mL) finely chopped
    flat-leaf parsley

This recipe for creamed cauliflower will have you questioning why you've always made mashed potatoes. Cauliflower is a perfect match for this beef filet basted with thyme and garlic butter—or for any other cut of meat you choose!

THYME and GARLIC BUTTER BASTED BEEF FILETS with CAULIFLOWER PURÉE

Serves 2

Cauliflower Purée

4 cups (1 L) cauliflower florets (about ½ head)
1 medium white onion, diced
2 cups (500 mL) heavy (35%) cream
2 sprigs thyme
Kosher salt and cracked black pepper

Red Wine Mushrooms

3 tablespoons (45 mL) unsalted butter
3 cups (750 mL) thickly sliced mixed mushrooms
2 tablespoons (30 mL) minced shallot
¼ cup (60 mL) dry red wine
½ cup (125 mL) beef stock
1 tablespoon (15 mL) finely chopped chives
Kosher salt and cracked black pepper

Beef Filets

2 beef filets (about 6 ounces/170 g each)
Kosher salt and cracked black pepper
1 tablespoon (15 mL) olive oil
2 tablespoons (30 mL) unsalted butter
2 cloves garlic, peeled and smashed
2 sprigs thyme

Make the Cauliflower Purée

1. In a medium saucepan over medium heat, combine cauliflower, onion, cream and thyme. Bring to a boil, then reduce heat to medium-low, cover, and cook for 5 minutes.

2. Remove lid and continue cooking until most of the cooking liquid is absorbed and cauliflower is tender. Discard thyme sprigs, then finely mash cauliflower. Season to taste with salt and pepper and keep warm until ready to serve.

Make the Red Wine Mushrooms

3. In a large skillet over medium-high heat, melt butter. Add mushrooms and shallots and sauté until mushrooms begin to brown, about 15 minutes, stirring often. Add wine and cook until liquid evaporates, then add stock and cook until sauce is thick enough to coat the back of a spoon. Remove from heat, stir in chives, and season to taste with salt and pepper. Keep warm.

Prepare the Beef Filets

4. Pat filets dry with paper towel and season well with salt and pepper. In a skillet over high heat, heat oil. Add filets and cook until browned on the bottom, about 3 minutes. Reduce heat to medium-high, turn filets over and cook 3 minutes more for medium-rare doneness.

5. Add butter, garlic and thyme and baste filets for 1 minute. Turn over and baste other side for 1 minute more. Transfer filets to a plate, tent with foil and let rest for 5 minutes before serving.

6. To serve, spoon Cauliflower Purée onto each plate. Top with a filet and Red Wine Mushrooms. Drizzle with some extra mushroom pan sauce and serve immediately.

CELERY

Celery is so often used but rarely given the proper shout-out it deserves. All those reasons we might overlook it—its mild green flavour and watery crunch—are the very reasons to celebrate this most underrated vegetable. I love a simple crudité platter with ranch dressing and celery for dipping, but there's so much more to celery. It has become a shining star in many of my recipes, including my Cashew Chicken Stir-Fry with Celery and Bean Sprouts, where it adds freshness, colour and texture. And really, what would any respectable tuna salad sandwich be without our good friend?

CELERY ROOT

Celery root, also known as celeriac, is a type of celery cultivated for its root. It looks intimidating, but when its knobby exterior is peeled away, this pale, ivory-coloured, dense root can be used in so many ways. I consider it one of the most versatile vegetables in the colder months. It has an incredible silkiness when puréed into a soup, and you don't need potatoes to make the best mash—a delicious alternative is my Celery Root Purée with Celery Leaf Pesto. But I love celery root most when it's grated raw into a wintery salad, giving the simplest combination of ingredients such depth of flavour and texture.

It's Sunday night, why not order in Chinese! That's what we always did at home when I was a kid. This is my version of comforting cashew chicken: a wok filled with tender stir-fried chicken, lots of celery, bean sprouts and roasted cashews, all bathed in a garlicky ginger sauce that tastes way better than takeout.

CASHEW CHICKEN STIR-FRY with CELERY and BEAN SPROUTS

Serves 4

2 tablespoons (30 mL) soy sauce, divided
1 teaspoon (5 mL) minced red and yellow chili
1 teaspoon (5 mL) grated peeled fresh ginger
1 teaspoon (5 mL) minced garlic
Grated zest of 1 orange
1 pound (450 g) boneless, skinless chicken thighs, each thigh cut into 4 pieces
1 tablespoon (15 mL) canola oil
2 ribs celery, thinly sliced on the diagonal
¼ cup (60 mL) thinly sliced shallots
½ cup (125 mL) chicken stock
Juice of 1 orange
1 tablespoon (15 mL) cornstarch
2 cups (500 mL) bean sprouts
¼ cup (60 mL) roasted cashews
¼ cup (60 mL) celery leaves
Cilantro leaves, for garnish

1. In a large bowl, stir together 1 tablespoon (15 mL) soy sauce, chili, ginger, garlic and orange zest until combined. Add chicken and stir to coat. Cover and let marinate for 30 minutes in the refrigerator.

2. In a wok or large skillet over high heat, heat oil to smoking point. Add chicken and stir-fry until golden, about 3 minutes. Add celery and shallots and stir-fry for 2 minutes. Add stock and orange juice and reduce by half.

3. Stir together cornstarch and remaining 1 tablespoon (15 mL) soy sauce until blended. Add to wok and stir-fry until sauce thickens. Add bean sprouts, cashews and celery leaves and stir-fry 1 minute more.

4. Transfer to a serving bowl. Garnish with cilantro and serve immediately.

This recipe takes the classic tuna sandwich to a whole new level. I love the crunch and freshness of the celery with the creamy lemon caper aïoli. I also use lots of celery leaves, which is the key to making this more than just your regular deli-style tuna salad.

TUNA SALAD SANDWICH with CELERY HEARTS and LEMON CAPER AÏOLI

Make the Lemon Caper Aïoli

1. In a deep, narrow bowl, whisk together egg yolk, garlic, lemon zest and juice, capers, Worcestershire sauce and Sriracha until combined. Whisk in oil a few drops at a time until mixture thickens enough to coat the back of a spoon. Stir in parsley and season to taste with salt and pepper. Cover and refrigerate aïoli until ready to use.

Make the Tuna Salad

2. Place tuna in a bowl and mash with a fork. Add celery hearts and leaves and 2 tablespoons (30 mL) Lemon Caper Aïoli. Fold to combine. Season to taste with salt and pepper.

Assemble the Tuna Salad Sandwich

3. Place 3 romaine leaves on each slice of toast and spoon tuna salad on top. Garnish with celery leaves and serve immediately.

Serves 2

Lemon Caper Aïoli
Makes about ¼ cup (60 mL)
1 large egg yolk
1 clove garlic, mashed
Grated zest and juice of ½ lemon
1 tablespoon (15 mL) chopped capers
⅛ teaspoon (0.5 mL) Worcestershire sauce
⅛ teaspoon (0.5 mL) Sriracha sauce
¼ cup (60 mL) extra-virgin olive oil
1 tablespoon (15 mL) finely chopped flat-leaf parsley
Kosher salt and cracked black pepper

Tuna Salad
1 can (7 ounces/198 g) solid white tuna, drained
¼ cup (60 mL) finely chopped celery hearts and leaves
Kosher salt and cracked black pepper

To Serve
2 slices buttered toast
6 baby romaine lettuce leaves
1 tablespoon (15 mL) celery leaves

Celery root's charm lies in its delicate flavour, which is a cross between celery with a touch of fennel. It takes on a nutty warmth when cooked. It loves butter, cream and cheese. Celery leaf pesto is a vibrant addition to the creamy purée.

CELERY ROOT PURÉE with CELERY LEAF PESTO

Serves 6

Celery Leaf Pesto
Makes about ½ cup (125 mL)

1 cup (250 mL) packed celery leaves
½ cup (125 mL) flat-leaf parsley
    leaves
½ cup (125 mL) finely grated
    Parmesan cheese
¼ cup (60 mL) toasted pumpkin seeds
1 tablespoon (15 mL) lemon juice
1 teaspoon (5 mL) grated lemon zest
¼ cup (60 mL) extra-virgin olive oil
Kosher salt and cracked black pepper

Celery Root Purée

1 celery root (about 2½ pounds/
    1.125 kg), peeled and cut into
    1-inch (2.5 cm) cubes
¼ cup (60 mL) heavy (35%) cream
2 tablespoons (30 mL) unsalted butter
Kosher salt and cracked black pepper

Make the Celery Leaf Pesto

1. In a food processor, combine celery leaves, parsley, Parmesan, pumpkin seeds, lemon juice and zest. Process until combined. With processor running, slowly pour oil through feed tube and process until well combined, scraping down sides of bowl if necessary. Season to taste with salt and pepper and set aside.

Make the Celery Root Purée

2. Place celery root in a saucepan of lightly salted cold water and bring to a boil. Reduce heat to medium and cook until celery root is fork-tender, about 15 minutes.

3. Drain celery root well, then return to pot and mash with cream and butter until smooth. Season to taste with salt and pepper.

4. To serve, spoon purée into a warm bowl, make a well in the centre and fill with a few tablespoons of Celery Leaf Pesto. Serve immediately.

These ribs are finger-licking good. The award-winning combination of ingredients in the dry rub seasons up any rib perfectly. I always make a double batch of the glaze and serve some on the side. With the delicious lentil and celery root ragout, this makes for an incredibly comforting meal on a chilly autumn day.

HONEY GARLIC LAMB RIBS with LENTIL and CELERY ROOT RAGOUT

1. Preheat oven to 375°F (190°C).

Make the Honey Garlic Glaze

2. In a medium saucepan, combine honey, ginger, shallots, garlic and red pepper flakes. Cook over medium heat until mixture begins to bubble, about 3 minutes. Stir in soy sauce, mustard and Worcestershire sauce and cook for 2 minutes more. Transfer mixture to a blender, add cilantro and process until smooth. Set aside.

Make the Dry Rub and Prepare the Ribs

3. In a small bowl, combine paprika, cumin, coriander, fennel, sugar, and red pepper flakes. Season ribs with salt and pepper. Rub spice mixture all over the ribs and place on a wire rack set in a roasting pan. Cover with foil and bake ribs for 1 hour.

Make the Lentil and Celery Root Ragout

4. In a skillet over medium heat, heat oil. Add celery root and cook until golden, about 5 minutes, stirring often. Stir in lentils, cranberries and parsley and cook until thoroughly heated, about 5 minutes. Season to taste with salt and pepper. Keep warm.

5. After an hour in the oven, uncover the ribs and continue to cook until tender and internal temperature reaches 175°F (80°C), 10 to 15 minutes longer. Let rest for 5 minutes, then brush racks with Honey Garlic Glaze.

6. Divide ribs by cutting between the bones. Brush ribs with more Honey Garlic Glaze and serve with Lentil and Celery Root Ragout.

Serves 4

3 to 4 pounds (1.35 to 1.8 kg) lamb ribs

Honey Garlic Glaze
¾ cup (175 mL) honey
2 tablespoons (30 mL) finely chopped peeled fresh ginger
2 tablespoons (30 mL) finely chopped shallots
2 tablespoons (30 mL) finely chopped garlic
1 teaspoon (5 mL) red pepper flakes
3 tablespoons (45 mL) soy sauce
2 tablespoons (30 mL) Dijon mustard
1 teaspoon (5 mL) Worcestershire sauce
⅓ cup (75 mL) cilantro leaves

Dry Rub
1½ teaspoons (7 mL) smoked paprika
1¼ teaspoons (6 mL) ground cumin
1 teaspoon (5 mL) ground coriander
½ teaspoon (2 mL) ground fennel seeds
½ teaspoon (2 mL) granulated sugar
¼ teaspoon (1 mL) red pepper flakes
Kosher salt and cracked black pepper

Lentil and Celery Root Ragout
2 tablespoons (30 mL) canola oil
1 cup (250 mL) diced peeled celery root
1 can (19 ounces/540 mL) lentils, drained and rinsed
2 tablespoons (30 mL) sun-dried cranberries
1 tablespoon (15 mL) finely chopped flat-leaf parsley
Kosher salt and cracked black pepper

One of the first recipes I ever learned how to make as a young chef in Montreal was celeriac rémoulade, a French classic. I fell in love with this delicious crisp, raw salad of celery root tossed with a mayonnaise, lemon and Dijon mustard dressing, and this remains my favourite way to prepare celery root. Here, I celebrate smoked salmon's light cedar and smoky flavours by enhancing it with the earthiness of grated celery root and the crisp sweetness of apples. This dish makes for a flawless Sunday brunch starter with warm toasted bagels.

SMOKED SALMON with CELERY ROOT and APPLE RÉMOULADE

Serves 4

½ cup (125 mL) coarsely grated peeled celery root
1 red apple, cored and julienned
2 teaspoons (10 mL) finely diced dill pickle
3 tablespoons (45 mL) mayonnaise
1 tablespoon (15 mL) whole-grain mustard (I like Kozlik's Triple Crunch Mustard)
Kosher salt and cracked black pepper
5 ounces (140 g) sliced wild sockeye smoked salmon
2 tablespoons (30 mL) coarsely chopped dill

1. In a bowl, fold together celery root, apple, pickle, mayonnaise and mustard until well combined. Season to taste with salt and pepper. Set rémoulade aside.

2. Fan salmon slices on serving platter. Top with rémoulade and dill and serve immediately.

FALL GREENS

Fall greens are not only nutritious, they are great value. Big curly bunches of kale and colourful Swiss chard are sturdy, stubborn almost, and ready for a good match. For this reason, fall greens are perfectly suited to our blustery Canadian autumn. They're wonderful for braising and for stirring into a pot with hearty, rustic flavours. You need a bit of gusto in a cold-weather soup, and the greens in my Kale, Bean and Squash Minestrone provide that healthy body. Speaking of nutrition, I've got two winning superfood salads—Kale Salad with Falafel Croutons and Sumac Vinaigrette and a Warm Swiss Chard Salad with Pancetta, Raisins and Pine Nuts—that can both be eaten as complete meals thanks to their hearty greens.

The taste of minestrone soup can change so dramatically depending on the season. In the fall I add lots of hearty greens and butternut squash. It's worth making an extra batch of the kale pesto to have on hand. It's a wonderful addition to this soup, and you'll find it equally delicious tossed with pasta and chili oil for a quick weeknight dinner, or spread on toast and topped with a fried egg for a speedy and effortless breakfast.

KALE, BEAN and SQUASH MINESTRONE

Serves 6 to 8

Kale Pesto

Makes about 1½ cups (375 mL)

1 cup (250 mL) packed stemmed and torn kale
½ cup (125 mL) packed fresh basil leaves
1 teaspoon (5 mL) sea salt
¼ cup (60 mL) extra-virgin olive oil
¼ cup (60 mL) toasted walnuts
2 cloves garlic, chopped
½ cup (125 mL) grated Parmesan cheese

Kale, Bean and Squash Minestrone

2 tablespoons (30 mL) olive oil
2 cups (500 mL) chopped leeks, white and light green parts only
2 teaspoons (10 mL) kosher salt
2 tablespoons (30 mL) minced garlic
3 cups (750 mL) diced peeled butternut squash
4 cups (1 L) packed stemmed and chopped kale
2 sprigs rosemary
6 cups (1.5 L) chicken stock
1 can (19 ounces/540 mL) white kidney beans, drained and rinsed
2 cups (500 mL) cooked pasta, such as ditalini or small elbow macaroni

To Serve

½ cup (125 mL) grated Parmesan cheese
2 tablespoons (30 mL) chopped flat-leaf parsley

Make the Kale Pesto

1. In a food processor, combine kale, basil and salt. Pulse until kale is finely chopped. With processor running, drizzle in olive oil. Add walnuts and garlic and process again, then add Parmesan and pulse to combine. Set aside. (You can keep leftover pesto in a covered jar in the refrigerator for up to 1 month.)

Make the Kale, Bean and Squash Minestrone

2. In a large saucepan over medium heat, heat oil. Add leeks and salt and cook until translucent, about 5 minutes, stirring frequently. Add garlic and cook for 1 minute more. Add squash, kale, rosemary and stock and cook until squash is tender, about 20 minutes, stirring occasionally.

3. Remove rosemary sprigs. Add beans and pasta and heat thoroughly.

4. Ladle soup into warmed bowls. Top each serving with about 1½ teaspoons (7 mL) Kale Pesto. Sprinkle with Parmesan and parsley and serve immediately.

Swiss chard is a beautiful green, and bacon makes everything better. In this salad the chard and the salty pancetta are sautéed together and then combined with sweet golden raisins and perfectly toasted pine nuts at the last minute, bringing that crunchy, over-the-top nutty taste. This salad is wonderful served with crispy-skinned roasted chicken and warm bread.

WARM SWISS CHARD SALAD with PANCETTA, RAISINS and PINE NUTS

1. Separate stems from chard leaves and finely chop. Tear chard leaves into large pieces. Set aside separately.

2. Cut bread into ¼-inch (5 mm) cubes. Set aside.

3. In a skillet over medium heat, heat oil. Add pancetta and fry for about 5 minutes, until crisp and golden. With a slotted spoon, transfer pancetta to paper towel to drain.

4. Add 1 tablespoon (15 mL) butter to the skillet. Add bread cubes and fry until crisp and golden, about 5 minutes, stirring often. Transfer croutons to paper towel to drain.

5. Add reserved chard stems, garlic and raisins to the skillet and cook until stems are tender, about 5 minutes, stirring often. Transfer mixture to a bowl.

6. Melt remaining 1 tablespoon (15 mL) butter in the skillet. Add reserved chard leaves and cook until barely wilted. Add lemon juice and parsley and continue cooking until liquid evaporates, about 2 minutes more. Toss in reserved pancetta and croutons and season to taste with salt and pepper.

7. Place chard leaves on a warmed serving platter, top with chard stem mixture, sprinkle with pine nuts and serve immediately.

Serves 4

1 bunch Swiss chard
2 slices pumpernickel bread
1 tablespoon (15 mL) canola oil
4 ounces (115 g) pancetta, diced
2 tablespoons (30 mL) unsalted
    butter, divided
1 clove garlic, chopped
⅓ cup (75 mL) golden raisins
Juice of ½ lemon
1 tablespoon (15 mL) finely chopped
    flat-leaf parsley
Kosher salt and cracked black pepper
2 tablespoons (30 mL) toasted pine
    nuts

This salad is a perfect meal for lunch or dinner. It is incredibly satisfying, with its mixture of seeds and nuts, earthy kale, nutty farro, feta cheese and crispy falafel croutons. This recipe makes a few extra falafels to store in the freezer, to pull out for your soon-to-be-favourite salad.

KALE SALAD with FALAFEL CROUTONS and SUMAC VINAIGRETTE

Serves 4

Falafel Croutons
Makes 10 to 12 pieces
1 cup (250 mL) cooked or canned
   chickpeas
½ small yellow onion, chopped
2 tablespoons (30 mL) chopped
   flat-leaf parsley
2 tablespoons (30 mL) chopped cilantro
1 teaspoon (5 mL) baking powder
1 teaspoon (5 mL) ground cumin
1 teaspoon (5 mL) kosher salt
Grated zest and juice of 1 lemon
4 to 6 tablespoons (60 to 90 mL)
   chickpea flour
Vegetable oil, for deep-frying

Sumac Vinaigrette
2 tablespoons (30 mL) sherry vinegar
¼ cup (60 mL) olive oil
1 tablespoon (15 mL) pumpkin oil
2 teaspoons (10 mL) Dijon mustard
   (I like Kozlik's Amazing Maple
   Mustard)
½ teaspoon (2 mL) Worcestershire
   sauce
Grated zest and juice of ½ orange
1 teaspoon (5 mL) sumac
Pinch of cayenne

Kale Salad
4 cups (1 L) stemmed and finely
   chopped kale
1 cup (250 mL) cooked farro
1 cup (250 mL) cooked or canned
   chickpeas
¼ cup (60 mL) salted toasted
   pumpkin seeds
¼ cup (60 mL) sunflower seeds
¼ cup (60 mL) coarsely chopped
   toasted hazelnuts
Kosher salt and cracked black pepper
½ cup (125 mL) crumbled feta cheese

Make the Falafel Croutons
1. In a food processor, combine chickpeas, onion, parsley, cilantro, baking powder, cumin, salt and lemon zest and juice. Pulse until chopped. Add chickpea flour 1 tablespoon (15 mL) at a time, pulsing after each addition until a soft, pliable dough is achieved.

2. Divide dough into 10 to 12 equal pieces. Roll each piece into a ball, transferring to a plate. Cover with plastic wrap and refrigerate for at least half an hour.

3. Half fill a medium saucepan with oil and heat to 350°F (180°C). Working in batches, deep-fry falafel croutons until crisp and golden, 3 to 5 minutes, then transfer to paper towel to drain and season lightly with kosher salt.

Make the Sumac Vinaigrette
4. In a small bowl, combine vinegar, olive and pumpkin oils, mustard, Worcestershire sauce, orange zest and juice, sumac and cayenne. Whisk until blended.

Assemble the Kale Salad
5. In a large bowl, toss together kale, farro, chickpeas, pumpkin seeds, sunflower seeds and hazelnuts. Dress salad with Sumac Vinaigrette, toss well to coat, and season to taste with salt and pepper.

6. Spoon salad onto a serving platter. Tear 8 Falafel Croutons into small pieces. Top salad with Falafel Croutons and feta.

Saltimbocca means "jump in the mouth," and once you try this veal, you'll know why! This dish takes no time at all to prepare—a recipe that your family and friends will ask for over and over again. If you don't have veal, chicken cutlets work just as well, and it's delicious served with my Cauliflower Pasta with Pecorino and Rosemary (page 34).

VEAL SALTIMBOCCA with SAUTÉED SPINACH

Prepare the Veal Saltimbocca

1. Season veal cutlets lightly with salt and pepper. Place 3 sage leaves in a single layer on top of each cutlet and cover with prosciutto.

2. In a large skillet over medium-high heat, heat canola oil until shimmering. Add veal prosciutto side down and sauté until golden, about 3 minutes. Flip over and cook for 1 minute more. Transfer to a plate.

3. Melt butter in the skillet. Add garlic and fry until golden, stirring frequently. Remove from heat, then add lemon juice, parsley and sage and swirl to coat. Set aside.

Make the Sautéed Spinach

4. Heat olive oil in another large skillet over high heat. Add spinach, garlic, salt and pepper. Cook, stirring rapidly, until spinach is wilted and most of the moisture has evaporated. Remove the garlic.

5. To serve, place sautéed spinach on serving platter. Set veal on top and spoon hot butter mixture over veal. Serve immediately.

Serves 2

Veal Saltimbocca
2 veal cutlets (about 4 ounces/115 g each)
Kosher salt and cracked black pepper
6 sage leaves
2 large slices prosciutto
1 tablespoon (15 mL) canola oil
2 tablespoons (30 mL) unsalted butter
2 cloves garlic, thinly sliced
1 tablespoon (15 mL) lemon juice
1 tablespoon (15 mL) chopped flat-leaf parsley
1 tablespoon (15 mL) chopped sage

Sautéed Spinach
2 tablespoons (30 mL) olive oil
4 to 6 cups (1 to 1.5 L) baby spinach, tough stems removed
1 clove garlic, thinly sliced
Kosher salt and cracked black pepper

GRAPES

In the fall, we like to take weekend trips out to the Niagara region, to see the spectacular leaves, of course, but also to visit the award-winning wineries in the area. Later, at the farmers' markets and roadside stands on the way home, inspired by our adventures, we'll pick up baskets of fresh, gorgeous grapes, in still-life-worthy velveteen bunches. We'll snack on them, tart and juicy, as we gather equipment to cook them at the restaurant—a pot for the season's Concord Grape Jelly; a baking sheet for the Balsamic Roasted Grape and Goat Cheese Bruschetta; a seasoned cast-iron pan for my decadent Foie Gras with Champagne Grapes. It's local and seasonal eating at its best.

Roasting grapes with thyme and balsamic vinegar makes them more savoury than sweet. They pair perfectly with the tang and creaminess of the goat cheese and make for a delicious bruschetta topping. I also use these roasted grapes on salads, and they make an incredible garnish for roasted lamb, chicken or earthy vegetables like carrots, beets or parsnips.

BALSAMIC ROASTED GRAPE and GOAT CHEESE BRUSCHETTA

1. Preheat oven to 350°F (180°C) and line a baking sheet with parchment paper.

2. Stir together goat cheese and cream until blended. Set aside.

3. In a large bowl, stir together grapes, thyme leaves, vinegar, honey, oil and ginger until combined. Spread in a single layer on the prepared baking sheet and roast until grapes start to blister, about 15 minutes. Transfer baking sheet to a wire rack and let grapes cool slightly.

4. While grapes are cooling, set oven to broil. Place bread on a second baking sheet and set 6 inches (15 cm) from broiler. Toast on both sides, about 2 to 3 minutes per side.

5. Smear goat cheese mixture onto bread slices. Top with warm grape mixture, sprinkle with pecans and season lightly with salt and pepper. Serve immediately.

Serves 4

1 cup (250 mL) soft goat cheese
2 to 3 tablespoons (30 to 45 mL) heavy (35%) cream
3 cups (750 mL) mixed seedless grapes, halved lengthwise
2 sprigs thyme, leaves only
1 tablespoon (15 mL) balsamic vinegar
1 tablespoon (15 mL) honey
2 teaspoons (10 mL) extra-virgin olive oil
½ teaspoon (2 mL) finely diced peeled fresh ginger
4 thick slices sourdough bread
½ cup (125 mL) finely chopped toasted pecans
Kosher salt and cracked black pepper

Despite their name, Champagne grapes aren't used to make the sparkling wine that I adore. Legend has it that they were so named because the tiny clusters of fruit resemble the bubbles in a glass of Champagne. I love how they look presented in perfect clusters atop the seared foie gras. These grapes have just the right balance of sweetness and acidity to complement this beautiful dish's richness and velvety texture.

FOIE GRAS with CHAMPAGNE GRAPES

Serves 2

2 tablespoons (30 mL) unsalted butter
2 slices brioche (2 inches/5 cm thick), crusts removed
¼ cup (60 mL) Concord Grape Jelly (see below)
¼ cup (60 mL) dry red wine
¼ cup (60 mL) sherry vinegar
⅓ cup (75 mL) granulated sugar
2 pieces foie gras (about 2 ounces/ 55 g each), cleaned and deveined
½ pound (225 g) Champagne grape clusters (about 2 clusters)
2 teaspoons (10 mL) Champagne grapes
Kosher salt and cracked black pepper

1. In a skillet over medium heat, melt butter. Add brioche and fry until golden brown on all sides. Transfer to paper towel and set aside.

2. In a small saucepan, combine jelly, wine, vinegar and sugar. Over medium-high heat, reduce by one-third, about 3 to 4 minutes, stirring often. The mixture should be thick enough to coat the back of a spoon. Keep sauce warm.

3. Heat the skillet over medium-high heat. Score foie gras in a cross-hatch pattern on both sides. Add to pan and sear until golden on both sides, turning only once, about 2 minutes per side. Transfer to a plate. Add grape clusters to the skillet and very gently roll them in the duck fat until they glisten, about 30 seconds. Remove from pan.

4. To serve, drizzle reserved sauce on warmed plates. Set a brioche crouton in the centre of each plate, then top with a piece of foie gras and a grape cluster. Season lightly with salt and pepper. Garnish with Champagne grapes and serve immediately.

Concord grapes have a wonderful dark purple jacket, and it's their distinctive colour and flavour that make them one of the best grapes for juice and jelly. Grape jelly is a pantry staple, but this homemade version tastes nothing like what you buy at the supermarket. Once you start making your own, you won't want anything else.

CONCORD GRAPE JELLY

Makes six 1-pint (500 mL) jars

5 pounds (2.25 kg) grapes, such as Concord or Red Flame, stems removed
¼ cup (60 mL) water
4 cups (1 L) granulated sugar
3 tablespoons (45 mL) lemon juice
6 ounces (170 g) liquid pectin

1. Combine grapes and water in a large saucepan. Cover and gently cook over low heat for 5 minutes, until the juices start to run. Take a potato masher or fork and mash up the grapes. Cook, uncovered, for about 10 minutes more.

2. Place cheesecloth in a sieve set over a bowl. Pour grape mixture into the cheesecloth and let it drip through for at least 1 hour or preferably overnight. Do not press on the grape mixture or your jelly will be cloudy.

3. Measure out the juice (you should have about 4 cups/1 L) and pour it into a pot with the sugar and lemon juice. Set the pan over high heat and bring to a boil. Stir in liquid pectin. Let the mixture boil for 5 minutes, skimming any foam.

4. Pour the hot jelly into sterilized jars. Keep refrigerated for up to 3 months.

The combination of peanut butter and chocolate is one of the most delicious discoveries. This adult version of a pudding cup is a perfect marriage of creamy peanut butter, smooth and decadent chocolate and a wicked punch of grape jelly!

PEANUT BUTTER POTS DE CRÈME with GRAPE JELLY and SPONGE TOFFEE

Serves 8

Sponge Toffee
2½ cups (625 mL) granulated sugar
⅔ cup (150 mL) light corn syrup
⅓ cup (75 mL) water
4 teaspoons (20 mL) baking soda
1 tablespoon (15 mL) pure vanilla
　extract

Peanut Butter Pots de Crème
2 cups (500 mL) heavy (35%) cream
½ cup (125 mL) whole milk
¾ cup (175 mL) creamy peanut butter
½ cup (125 mL) semisweet chocolate
　chips
6 large egg yolks
⅓ cup (75 mL) granulated sugar

To Serve
½ cup (125 mL) Concord Grape Jelly
　(page 64)

Make the Sponge Toffee

1. Grease and line with foil a 13- × 9-inch (3.5 L) cake pan.

2. In a large saucepan over medium heat, stir together sugar, corn syrup and water just until sugar dissolves. Bring to a boil, then cook without stirring but brushing down side of pan occasionally with pastry brush dipped in cold water, until a candy thermometer reaches the hard-crack stage of 300°F (150°C), or when 1 teaspoon (5 mL) hot syrup dropped into cold water forms hard, brittle threads, about 10 minutes.

3. Remove from heat and whisk in baking soda. Be careful, as the caramel will bubble and sputter and increase in volume. Stir in vanilla.

4. Pour into the prepared pan. Let cool in pan on a wire rack, without disturbing, for about 2 hours. Break into 1½-inch (4 cm) pieces. (Sponge toffee can be stored, layered between waxed paper in an airtight container, for up to 1 month.)

Make the Peanut Butter Pots de Crème

5. Preheat oven to 325°F (160°C).

6. In a medium saucepan, combine cream and milk. Bring to a simmer over medium heat, then remove from heat and stir in peanut butter and chocolate chips until melted and smooth.

7. In a medium bowl, whisk together egg yolks and sugar until thick and pale. Gradually add hot cream mixture to egg mixture, whisking constantly so the eggs do not cook.

8. Pour the mixture into eight 4-ounce (125 mL) ramekins and place in a deep baking pan. Pour in enough hot water to come halfway up the sides of the ramekins. Bake for about 45 minutes, until the custard is just set.

9. Remove ramekins from the water bath and allow them to cool to room temperature. Chill for at least 2 hours before serving.

10. To serve, top Peanut Butter Pots de Crème with jelly and Sponge Toffee.

Back in the 1950s, the gin fizz was the most fashionable cocktail in Paris. My twist is to add Concord grape juice and St. Germain elderflower liqueur with its intoxicating lychee-pear taste. This refreshing cocktail is worthy of a celebration—and may just take you back in time!

GRAPE ELDERFLOWER GIN FIZZ

Serves 1

1 ounce (30 mL) gin
½ ounce (15 mL) St. Germain elderflower liqueur
¼ cup (60 mL) Concord grape juice
Juice of ½ lime
Club soda
Champagne grape cluster, for garnish

1. Fill a cocktail shaker with ice, then add gin, elderflower liqueur, grape juice and lime juice. Shake for about 15 seconds.

2. Strain into an ice-filled highball glass and top with a splash of soda. Garnish with grapes.

LEEKS

In the onion kingdom, the mighty leek is the undisputed emperor. It's got it all—a positively aristocratic heritage (Confit Leeks Vinaigrette Salad is a true classic recipe if there ever was one) but also an earthiness that is so easy to love. It provides elegant flavour to soups and is dreamy when softened in generous pats of butter. Yet it's also gutsy enough to take a grilling and stand up to bigger, richer flavours that would overwhelm lesser onion varieties. A bonus—thinly sliced and deep-fried crunchy-crispy slivers are addictive.

You can always find leeks in my kitchen. They have a milder onion flavour and are the foundation for many delicious soups, stews and pastas. When cutting the leeks for this recipe, use only the white and very light green parts, which will melt in your mouth. The darker green leaves take longer to cook and don't break down as nicely as the white parts, but you can save them for stocks and braises.

CONFIT LEEKS VINAIGRETTE SALAD

Serves 4

Confit Leeks
4 large leeks
2 bay leaves
½ serrano chili, thinly sliced into rounds
1 teaspoon (5 mL) fresh thyme leaves
1 teaspoon (5 mL) yellow mustard seeds
1½ to 2 cups (375 to 500 mL) canola or olive oil

Leek Vinaigrette
1 tablespoon (15 mL) whole-grain mustard (I like Kozlik's Triple Crunch Mustard)
Grated zest and juice of 1 lemon
Kosher salt and cracked black pepper

To Serve
4 cups (1 L) watercress
½ cup (125 mL) celery leaves

Make the Confit Leeks

1. Preheat oven to 325°F (160°C).

2. Trim and discard root end and outer layers from leeks, then slice white and light green parts crosswise into 1-inch (2.5 cm) rounds. Arrange in a single layer cut side up in a 2-quart (2 L) baking dish. Place bay leaves on top and sprinkle with chili, thyme and mustard seeds. Add enough oil to cover leeks.

3. Cover dish with foil and bake until leeks are fork-tender, about 90 minutes.

4. Transfer baking dish to a wire rack and let cool to room temperature. Carefully place cooled leeks in a bowl. Do not discard the remaining oil mixture.

Make the Leek Vinaigrette

5. Spoon ½ cup (125 mL) oil mixture from baking dish into a bowl. Add mustard, lemon zest and juice and whisk to combine. Season to taste with salt and pepper.

6. To serve, place watercress on a platter and arrange Confit Leeks on top. Sprinkle with celery leaves and drizzle with Leek Vinaigrette.

The rich saltiness of the roasted marrow in this dish is like spreading delicious beef-flavoured butter on toast topped with a fresh salsa. Salsa verde, the classic green sauce of Italy, is a combination of olive oil and chopped parsley flavoured with lemon zest, garlic and capers. I have my own take on this classic, adding lots of dill, olives and confit leeks, which will perk up anything, including steak, poultry and fish.

BONE MARROW and LEEK SALSA VERDE

1. Preheat oven to 375°F (190°C).

Make the Leek Salsa Verde

2. In a small bowl, stir together chives, dill, parsley, olives, confit leeks, olive oil and capers until combined. Season to taste with salt and pepper. Let salsa rest for at least 20 minutes to allow flavours to meld.

Prepare the Frizzled Leeks

3. Cut white and light green parts of leek crosswise into 3-inch (8 cm) pieces. Halve pieces lengthwise, then thinly slice into matchsticks. Toss lightly in cornstarch.

4. Half fill a small saucepan with oil and heat to 375°F (190°C). Fry leeks in batches until light golden brown and crispy, about 1 to 2 minutes. Transfer to paper towel to drain and season lightly with salt.

Prepare the Bone Marrow

5. Place marrow bones cut side up on a baking sheet and roast until marrow is softened, about 15 minutes. Set oven to broil and broil marrow until golden, about 2 minutes more.

6. To serve, place a bone marrow cut side up on each plate. Spoon Leek Salsa Verde over top and garnish with Frizzled Leeks, sea salt and fresh pepper. Serve immediately.

Serves 4

Leek Salsa Verde
¼ cup (60 mL) finely chopped chives
¼ cup (60 mL) finely chopped dill
¼ cup (60 mL) finely chopped flat-leaf parsley
¼ cup (60 mL) coarsely chopped pitted black and green olives
¼ cup (60 mL) chopped Confit Leeks (see page 70)
2 tablespoons (30 mL) olive oil
1 tablespoon (15 mL) capers
Kosher salt and cracked black pepper

Frizzled Leeks
1 leek, root and outer layers discarded
2 tablespoons (30 mL) cornstarch
Vegetable oil, for deep-frying
Kosher salt

Bone Marrow
2 marrow bones (5 inches/12 cm each), split lengthwise in half

To Serve
Maldon sea salt and cracked black pepper

MUSHROOMS

When the days start getting shorter and colder and my appetite turns to hearty, warming things, I can't help but crave grounding, sturdy dishes like stews, roasts and braises. In the fall I often look for satisfying meatiness while keeping things in the vegetable arena. This, my friends, is where the incredible mushroom comes in. They're rich and intensely flavoured without being heavy, and add incredible meaty texture to dishes that need a little earthiness. The secret to unlocking all that amazing flavour? High heat, a little patience to get things deeply roasted, and a trusty cast-iron pan go a long way.

Thick slices of sourdough bread toasted in butter—plenty of it—topped with a big spoonful of creamy hot mushrooms is a brunch comfort dish or appetizer that always pleases. I love topping this dish with a poached egg or crispy prosciutto.

CREAMY MUSHROOMS on SOURDOUGH TOAST

Fry the Sourdough Toast

1. In a large skillet over medium heat, melt butter. Fry bread until golden on both sides, about 2 minutes per side. Remove from pan and keep warm.

Make the Creamy Mushrooms

2. In the skillet over medium-high heat, melt butter and add oil. Add shallots and sauté until translucent. Add mushrooms and thyme and continue cooking until mushrooms release their juices and liquid evaporates, stirring frequently. Stir in lemon juice and cream until combined. Season to taste with salt and pepper.

3. Spoon Creamy Mushrooms over warm toast, garnish with parsley and serve immediately.

Serves 2

Sourdough Toast
2 tablespoons (30 mL) unsalted butter
2 slices sourdough bread
   (1 inch/2.5 cm thick)

Creamy Mushrooms
2 tablespoons (30 mL) unsalted butter
2 tablespoons (30 mL) olive oil
¼ cup (60 mL) finely diced shallots
4 cups (1 L) coarsely chopped
   assorted mushrooms
1 teaspoon (5 mL) fresh thyme leaves
½ teaspoon (2 mL) lemon juice
½ cup (125 mL) heavy (35%) cream
Kosher salt and cracked black pepper
1 tablespoon (15 mL) coarsely torn
   flat-leaf parsley

This is one of my favourite late-night snacks and a go-to quick fix for a chef after a long day in the kitchen—or for anyone after a long day. You want something easy and satisfying, and for me, an egg dish is comforting and fulfilling. Then again, I also love this dish for breakfast!

MUSHROOM FRIED RICE with CRISPY GINGER EGG

Serves 2

Mushroom Fried Rice

2 tablespoons (30 mL) olive oil

1 cup (250 mL) mushrooms, such as
    king oyster, cut lengthwise into
    ¼-inch (5 mm) slices

1 tablespoon (15 mL) unsalted butter

1 cup (250 mL) chopped leeks, white
    and light green parts only

2 cloves garlic, minced

1 teaspoon (5 mL) grated peeled fresh
    ginger

2 cups (500 mL) cooked purple
    jasmine rice

2 tablespoons (30 mL) soy sauce

2 green onions, thinly sliced on the
    diagonal

Crispy Ginger Eggs

6 tablespoons (90 mL) panko bread
    crumbs

2 teaspoons (10 mL) grated peeled
    fresh ginger

2 tablespoons (30 mL) unsalted
    butter, divided

2 large eggs

Make the Mushroom Fried Rice

1. In a large skillet over medium-high heat, heat oil until shimmering. Add mushrooms and cook until golden, about 3 minutes, turning often. Transfer to a plate and set aside.

2. To skillet add butter, leeks, garlic, ginger, rice and soy sauce. Stir-fry for 2 minutes. Add green onions and stir-fry for 1 minute more. Remove from heat and keep rice warm while frying eggs.

Make the Crispy Ginger Eggs

3. In a small bowl, stir together panko and ginger. Set aside.

4. In a small nonstick skillet over medium heat, melt 1 tablespoon (15 mL) butter. Spoon 3 tablespoons (45 mL) panko mixture into centre of pan and use the back of the spoon to flatten. Fry until bottom is golden and slightly crispy, then crack egg on top and cook until white has set, about 2 minutes more. Repeat with remaining egg.

5. Divide Mushroom Fried Rice between warmed plates, set Crispy Ginger Eggs on top and serve immediately.

PEARS

A ripe pear is an elegant thing, isn't it? Plump curves and all, it's no wonder we can't get enough of them when they come into season in the early fall. The easiest way to enjoy them is freshly picked, casually eaten out of hand or very simply sliced into cold wedges. Cooked, they become beautifully translucent and syrupy, perfect for balancing the deeper mellow flavours of fall. I'm a fan of serving them in savoury dishes, braised, poached or roasted; I think you'll love them in my Cornish Hen Braised with Pear and Endive. They also add a lovely body and sophisticated sweetness to richer meat dishes and robust salads, like my Pear and Blue Cheese Salad with Tamarind Vinaigrette.

This salad has bold flavours—bitter, sweet, salty and just a hint of a bright, citrusy tang from the vinaigrette. The tamarind is the secret ingredient and really enhances the flavours in this salad. Not only wonderful in this dish, tamarind is a fantastic addition to curries, marinades, desserts and even cocktails.

PEAR and BLUE CHEESE SALAD with TAMARIND VINAIGRETTE

Make the Tamarind Vinaigrette

1. In a small bowl, whisk together cider, olive and walnut oils, tamarind paste and honey until blended. Season to taste with salt and pepper. Set aside.

Prepare the Pear and Blue Cheese Salad

2. In a small skillet over medium heat, heat olive oil and butter. Add pear slices and cook until golden on both sides. Remove from heat.

3. Place frisée, grapes and walnuts in a large bowl and toss with ⅓ cup (75 mL) Tamarind Vinaigrette. Season well with salt and pepper.

4. Divide salad onto plates and top each with pear wedges. Garnish with blue cheese and serve.

Serves 4

Tamarind Vinaigrette
½ cup (125 mL) pressed sweet pear cider
½ cup (125 mL) olive oil
2 tablespoons (30 mL) walnut oil
2 tablespoons (30 mL) tamarind paste
2 tablespoons (30 mL) honey
Kosher salt and cracked black pepper

Pear and Blue Cheese Salad
1 tablespoon (15 mL) olive oil
1 tablespoon (15 mL) unsalted butter
2 large red Anjou pears, halved lengthwise, cored and cut into ¼-inch (5 mm) slices
4 cups (1 L) frisée leaves
½ cup (125 mL) mixed seedless grapes
¼ cup (60 mL) toasted walnut halves
½ cup (125 mL) crumbled blue cheese

My grandfather lived in St. Catharines, Ontario, and had a pear tree in his backyard; it was squat and old, but gave us the most delicious, little pears for many years. One of the first things we'd do after picking the fruit was make these simple fritters. They're best served piping hot, ideally with a strong afternoon coffee.

PEAR FRITTERS with CINNAMON SUGAR

1. In a deep bowl, whisk egg. Add flour, ¼ cup (60 mL) sugar, baking powder and cider and whisk until blended.

2. In a small bowl, stir together remaining ½ cup (125 mL) sugar and cinnamon until blended.

3. Half fill a small saucepan with oil and heat to 375°F (190°C). Working in batches, lightly dip pears into batter, place in hot oil and fry until crispy and golden, about 3 minutes per side. Transfer fritters to paper towel and sprinkle with cinnamon-sugar mixture. Serve immediately.

Serves 4

1 large egg
1½ cups (375 mL) all-purpose flour
¾ cup (175 mL) granulated sugar, divided
1 teaspoon (5 mL) baking powder
¾ cup (175 mL) pressed sweet pear cider
½ teaspoon (2 mL) cinnamon
Vegetable oil, for deep-frying
2 Bartlett pears, cored and cut lengthwise into ½-inch (1 cm) slices

A cousin of chicory, endive also has a slightly bitter taste. Here it is braised with sweet pears and a touch of sugar to balance out any bitterness, making it perfect served alongside Cornish hen.

CORNISH HEN BRAISED with PEAR and ENDIVE

Serves 4

2 Bosc pears, quartered, seeds removed
½ cup (125 mL) white wine, such as Riesling
¼ cup (60 mL) dark brown sugar
Grated zest and juice of 1 orange
4 sprigs sage
2 tablespoons (30 mL) olive oil
2 Cornish hens, each cut in half, backbone removed
Kosher salt and cracked black pepper
3 endives, cut lengthwise into quarters
3 cups (750 mL) chicken stock
3 tablespoons (45 mL) unsalted butter
2 tablespoons (30 mL) chopped flat-leaf parsley

1. Preheat oven to 350°F (180°C).

2. Place pears, wine, brown sugar, orange zest and juice and sage in a bowl. Toss together and allow to marinate for 30 minutes.

3. Heat a large ovenproof skillet over medium-high heat. Add oil. Season Cornish hens with salt and pepper and place them in the pan skin side down. Cook until golden brown all over, 2 to 3 minutes per side. Transfer hens to a plate.

4. Remove pears from marinade, reserving marinade. To the skillet, add pears and endive and cook for 2 minutes, until caramelized.

5. Return hens to the pan. Add pear marinade and stock and bring to a boil. Season with salt and pepper.

6. Place the pan in the oven and cook for 25 to 30 minutes or until hens are cooked and pears are tender.

7. Using a slotted spoon, transfer hens, pears and endives to a serving dish. Return braising liquid to the stove over medium-high heat and reduce liquid to desired thickness. Whisk in butter and parsley and pour sauce over hens.

SWEET POTATOES

There's a whole digging-for-gold feeling when you're cooking with sweet potatoes, a pleasant sense of discovery that under an unassuming dusty-looking jacket lies quite the delicious treasure. And talk about a jackpot—I just can't get enough of that coppery orange colour and faintly buttery, almost malty sweet flavour. Sweet potatoes pair up perfectly with warm, earthy spices, like the nutmeg, cinnamon and black pepper in my Sweet Potato and Swiss Chard Moussaka. I'm also showing off their gorgeous sticky caramel quality by roasting them in my Twice-Baked Fully Loaded Sweet Potatoes.

A traditional moussaka this is not. I've started my own tradition with this spinoff. I use sweet potatoes instead of eggplant, and a lamb and Swiss chard filling with warm spice and savoury notes topped off with a pumpkin béchamel with lots of Parmesan cheese. This is a meal in itself or a great side dish at a family gathering.

SWEET POTATO and SWISS CHARD MOUSSAKA

Serves 8

Sweet Potatoes

3 to 4 large sweet potatoes (about 1 pound/450 g), peeled and cut into ¼-inch (5 mm) slices
2 tablespoons (30 mL) olive oil
2 sprigs thyme, leaves only
Kosher salt and cracked black pepper

Pumpkin Béchamel

¼ cup (60 mL) unsalted butter
¼ cup (60 mL) all-purpose flour
1 cup (250 mL) milk
1 teaspoon (5 mL) kosher salt
¼ teaspoon (1 mL) cracked black pepper
2 cups (500 mL) canned pumpkin purée
⅛ teaspoon (0.5 mL) freshly grated nutmeg
4 large egg yolks
½ cup (125 mL) grated Parmesan cheese

Lamb Filling

2 tablespoons (30 mL) extra-virgin olive oil, divided
1 pound (450 g) lean ground lamb
½ teaspoon (2 mL) cinnamon
⅛ teaspoon (0.5 mL) freshly grated nutmeg
1 cup (250 mL) finely chopped leeks, white part only
2 teaspoons (10 mL) minced garlic
4 cups (1 L) chopped Swiss chard leaves
1 teaspoon (5 mL) chopped thyme leaves
2 tablespoons (30 mL) chopped flat-leaf parsley

For Assembly

½ cup (125 mL) crumbled feta cheese

Make the Sweet Potatoes

1. Preheat oven to 375°F (190°C) and line a baking sheet with parchment paper.

2. Toss potatoes with oil and thyme leaves, and season well with salt and pepper. Place in a single layer on baking sheet. Bake until fork-tender, about 15 minutes, turning potatoes over halfway through baking time. Set aside.

Prepare the Pumpkin Béchamel

3. In a large saucepan over medium heat, melt butter. Add flour and cook until blended, stirring constantly. Whisk in milk, salt and pepper and cook until sauce begins to thicken, then whisk in pumpkin and nutmeg until blended. Remove from heat.

4. Transfer ½ cup (125 mL) béchamel to a small bowl and whisk in egg yolks 1 at a time. Whisk yolk mixture back into white sauce until blended. Stir in Parmesan. Keep warm.

Make the Lamb Filling

5. In a large skillet over medium heat, add 1 tablespoon (15 mL) oil, lamb, cinnamon and nutmeg. Cook lamb until browned, about 15 minutes, breaking meat up with the back of a spoon if necessary.

6. With a slotted spoon, transfer lamb mixture to a bowl. Discard any fat from skillet.

7. Return skillet to medium heat and add remaining 1 tablespoon (15 mL) oil and leeks. Sauté until leeks are translucent, about 5 minutes, stirring frequently. Add garlic, chard and thyme and cook until chard has wilted, about 5 minutes, stirring frequently. Stir in parsley and reserved lamb mixture until combined. Set aside to cool slightly.

Assemble and Bake the Moussaka

8. Preheat oven to 425°F (220°C) and butter a 2-quart (2 L) casserole dish.

9. Arrange Sweet Potato Planks over bottom of casserole, top with lamb mixture and sprinkle with feta. Spoon warm Pumpkin Béchamel over top and smooth with the back of a spoon.

10. Bake until thoroughly heated and golden brown, about 25 minutes. Let moussaka cool for 10 minutes before serving.

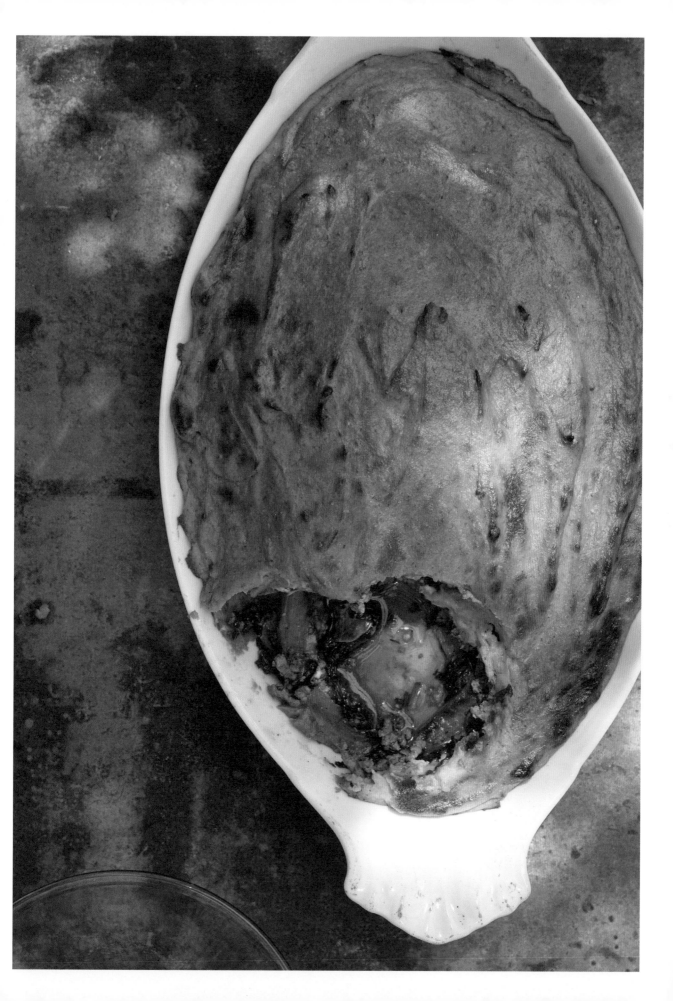

This recipe will turn anyone into a sweet potato lover. These little sweet potatoes filled with goat cheese, cheddar and green onions and topped with a spicy aïoli will make everyone reach back to the plate for seconds. I love serving this as a side dish or a canapé.

TWICE-BAKED FULLY LOADED SWEET POTATOES

1. Preheat oven to 350°F (180°C) and line a baking sheet with parchment paper.

2. Set sweet potatoes cut side up on the baking sheet and drizzle with olive oil. Roast until fork-tender, about 30 minutes.

3. Meanwhile, in a skillet over medium heat, fry bacon until crispy. Add shallot and cook until translucent, about 3 minutes, stirring often. Add green onions and cook until just wilted. Transfer mixture to a large bowl and set aside.

4. When cool enough to handle, scoop potato flesh into bowl with bacon mixture. Mash with a fork. Season to taste with salt and pepper.

5. Set oven to broil. Spoon filling back into potato skins. Top with goat cheese and cheddar. Broil until cheese melts, about 7 minutes. Drizzle with chipotle aïoli and serve immediately.

Serves 4

1 pound (450 g) mini sweet potatoes, scrubbed, patted dry and halved lengthwise
3 tablespoons (45 mL) olive oil
4 slices bacon, finely diced
1 small shallot, finely diced
1 bunch green onions, thinly sliced on the diagonal
Kosher salt and cracked black pepper
¼ cup (60 mL) crumbled soft goat cheese
¼ cup (60 mL) finely grated cheddar cheese
2 tablespoons (30 mL) Chipotle Aïoli (see page 128)

Brussels Sprouts
Cabbage
Garlic
Onions
Parsnips
Potatoes
Rutabaga
Squash
Sunchokes
Turnips

Winter

BRUSSELS SPROUTS

Truth be told, Brussels sprouts have had a bad rap. Forget those childhood memories of sad, over-boiled sprouts. When prepared well, they are incredibly delicious, and dare I say, addictive! I've found that a quick sear or sauté are key to bringing out the natural sweetness and bright personality of this misunderstood vegetable. Brussels sprouts also pair perfectly with smoky and salty flavours, like bacon in my simple Crispy Brussels Sprouts with Pancetta and Poached Eggs, and a good sharp pecorino cheese in my Brussels Sprout Leaves with Pecorino and Quinoa. For those of you still on the fence about one of my favourite vegetables, I promise these recipes will win over even the most doubtful.

After I visited Louisiana recently, I had a newfound craving for a traditional Cajun and Creole dish known as dirty rice. It is so good! The rice is "spicy" from cayenne and black pepper and "dirty" from the chicken livers it is cooked with. I've swapped out the "holy trinity" of ingredients—green peppers, celery and onions—for leeks, roasted Brussels sprouts and green onions . . . and lots of jalapeños.

BRUSSELS SPROUTS DIRTY RICE with ROASTED JALAPEÑOS and CHICKEN LIVERS

1. Preheat oven to 475°F (240°C) and line a baking sheet with parchment paper. In a small bowl, toss jalapeños with olive oil, salt and pepper. Lay peppers on the baking sheet and roast for 15 to 20 minutes, turning once, until skins are blistered. Let rest until cool enough to handle, then remove stem and seeds and finely chop.

2. In a large skillet over medium heat, heat canola oil. Add leeks, Brussels sprouts, garlic and roasted peppers and cook until leeks are tender and Brussels sprouts have started to brown, about 10 minutes, stirring often.

3. Push Brussels sprout mixture to edge of skillet and melt butter in centre. Add chicken livers and cook until thoroughly cooked, about 5 minutes.

4. Add rice and green onions and toss with vegetables and chicken livers to combine. Continue cooking until heated through and Brussels sprouts are golden brown, about 5 minutes more, stirring frequently. Season to taste with salt and pepper and serve immediately.

Serves 4

2 jalapeño peppers
1½ teaspoons (7 mL) olive oil
Kosher salt and cracked black pepper
2 tablespoons (30 mL) canola oil
1 cup (250 mL) diced leeks, white and pale green part only
1 cup (250 mL) shaved Brussels sprouts
1 teaspoon (5 mL) minced garlic
2 tablespoons (30 mL) unsalted butter
4 ounces (115 g) chicken livers, trimmed and coarsely chopped
2 cups (500 mL) cooked basmati rice
2 green onions, thinly sliced on the diagonal

We all know Brussels sprouts have been making a comeback for a while now. The flavours of perfectly roasted Brussels sprouts is something to be savoured. They pair beautifully with the smoky flavours of pancetta, and their naturally sweet, nutty undertones are elevated by the perfectly poached egg.

CRISPY BRUSSELS SPROUTS with PANCETTA and POACHED EGGS

Serves 4

2 tablespoons (30 mL) olive oil
4 thinly sliced pancetta rounds
2 cups (500 mL) halved Brussels
    sprouts, trimmed
2 tablespoons (30 mL) unsalted butter
Kosher salt and cracked black pepper
2 tablespoons (30 mL) white vinegar
    or other mild vinegar
4 large eggs

1. Preheat oven to 325°F (160°C).

2. In a medium skillet over medium heat, heat oil. Add pancetta and fry until crisp and golden, turning once. Transfer to paper towel to drain.

3. Working in batches, place Brussels sprouts cut side down in skillet and fry until golden, 3 to 4 minutes. Flip and cook for another 3 to 4 minutes. Transfer browned Brussels sprouts to a baking sheet and keep warm in oven while frying the rest.

4. Return pancetta and Brussels sprouts to skillet, add butter and toss gently to combine. Discard any loose leaves. Season Brussels sprout mixture with salt and pepper to taste. Set aside and keep warm.

5. Fill a saucepan about two-thirds with water, add vinegar and bring to a boil. Turn the heat down but still keep at a rolling boil. Crack 1 egg into a small measuring cup. With a slotted spoon, swirl the water in one direction and carefully lower the egg into the water. Cook for 3 to 4 minutes for a firm white and a gooey but still runny yolk. Use the slotted spoon to remove the egg from the water and set on a plate lined with paper towel. Repeat with the remaining eggs. Lightly pat the eggs dry with a paper towel and season to taste with salt and pepper.

6. Divide Brussels sprouts mixture onto warmed plates. Top each serving with a pancetta round and poached egg and serve immediately.

This dish is filled with texture and overflowing with nutrients, thanks to the protein-packed quinoa. Adding the sharp and salty pecorino cheese transforms it into something spectacular.

BRUSSELS SPROUT LEAVES with PECORINO and QUINOA

1. Place quinoa in a fine-mesh sieve. Rinse thoroughly with cool water for about 2 minutes, then drain well.

2. Heat olive oil in a medium saucepan over medium-high heat. Add drained quinoa and cook, stirring often, for about 1 minute to let the water evaporate and toast the quinoa. Stir in water or stock and salt and bring to a rolling boil. Lower heat to a simmer, cover and cook for 10 to 12 minutes, until tender and almost all the liquid has been absorbed.

3. Remove from heat and let stand, covered, for 5 more minutes. Remove the lid and fluff quinoa gently with a fork. If any liquid remains in the bottom of the pan or if the quinoa is still a bit crunchy, return the pot to low heat and cook, covered, for another 5 minutes, until all the water has been absorbed. Set aside and keep warm.

4. In a large skillet over medium heat, melt butter. Add shallot and cook until translucent, about 3 minutes, stirring often. Add Brussels sprout leaves and thyme and cook until leaves are barely wilted, about 5 minutes, stirring frequently. Season to taste with salt and pepper.

5. Spoon quinoa into a serving bowl, then top with Brussels sprout mixture and pecorino. Serve immediately.

Serves 4

1 cup (250 mL) uncooked quinoa (any colour)
2 tablespoons (30 mL) olive oil
2 cups (500 mL) water or stock
½ teaspoon (2 mL) kosher salt
2 tablespoons (30 mL) unsalted butter
1 shallot, julienned lengthwise
2 cups (500 mL) Brussels sprout leaves
1 teaspoon (5 mL) chopped thyme leaves
Kosher salt and cracked black pepper
¼ cup (60 mL) finely grated pecorino cheese

CABBAGE

There are many more varieties of cabbage to choose
from other than the ordinary and familiar green one.
Red cabbage is similar in flavour to green but with
regal dark purple leaves. Napa cabbage are oblong
with thick, crisp stems and light-coloured frilly leaves.
And the savoy is so pretty with its deeply crinkled,
tender leaves. Bringing a whole cabbage into your
kitchen requires a bit of commitment, but if you do,
with a few ideas up your sleeve—and I've got some
delicious ones for you—you'll be happy you did. You
can eat it raw, pickle it, cook it, ferment it. I think you'll
love a few of my favourites, a Quick Kimchi and my
Cabbage Roll with Kielbasa and Sage.

This deluxe, supersized cabbage roll features garlicky, flavourful diced kielbasa and plenty of grated root vegetables folded into the filling. Cooked as a single large roll, it's a great all-in-one dish to feed a crowd!

CABBAGE ROLL with KIELBASA and SAGE

1. In a large skillet over medium heat, heat oil. Add grated root vegetables and cook until most of the liquid is absorbed, about 15 minutes, stirring frequently. Remove from heat and let mixture cool to room temperature.

2. Preheat oven to 350°F (180°C) and grease a baking sheet.

3. In a pot of boiling salted water, blanch cabbage leaves until barely tender, about 3 minutes. With a slotted spoon, carefully transfer leaves to a bowl of ice water to stop the cooking process. Drain leaves, pat dry with paper towel and set aside.

4. In a large bowl, mix together pork, kielbasa, yellow onion, garlic, green onions, chili, thyme and sage until combined. Stir in cooled root vegetables.

5. Beat together eggs and cream and fold into meat mixture along with rice, parsley and salt until combined.

6. Lay cabbage leaves in an overlapping layer on the baking sheet. Shape pork mixture into a loaf down the centre of cabbage, leaving a border at each short end. Bring leaves up to encase meat.

7. Cover cabbage roll with foil and bake until internal temperature reaches 160°F (70°C), about 1 hour. Let cabbage roll rest for 15 minutes before cutting into 1-inch (2.5 cm) slices and serving on top of warm marinara sauce.

Serves 8

2 tablespoons (30 mL) canola oil
4 cups (1 L) peeled and coarsely grated mixed root vegetables, such as celery root, turnip, carrot, rutabaga
10 large savoy cabbage leaves
1 pound (450 g) lean ground pork
½ cup (125 mL) finely diced kielbasa
½ cup (125 mL) finely diced yellow onion
2 cloves garlic, minced
2 green onions, thinly sliced
1 tablespoon (15 mL) minced Fresno chili
1 tablespoon (15 mL) minced thyme
1 tablespoon (15 mL) minced sage
2 large eggs
¼ cup (60 mL) heavy (35%) cream
½ cup (125 mL) cold cooked wild rice
½ cup (125 mL) finely chopped flat-leaf parsley
1 teaspoon (5 mL) kosher salt
2 cups (500 mL) warmed Homemade Marinara Sauce (see below)

This is my go-to recipe for a simple yet delicious tomato sauce. I like to make a double or even triple batch and store some in my freezer to pull out for a quick pasta dinner. Try to find San Marzano tomatoes, if you can; they are less acidic, making for a more balanced sauce.

HOMEMADE MARINARA SAUCE

1. Pour tomatoes and their juices into a large bowl and crush them with your hands. Pour 1 cup (250 mL) water into the can and swish it around to get all the tomato juices. Add this to the tomatoes.

2. In a large skillet, heat oil over medium heat. Add garlic, and as soon as it's sizzling, add tomatoes, red pepper flakes, salt and sugar. Stir together. Add basil sprigs and simmer sauce until thickened and oil on surface is a deep orange, about 15 minutes. Remove basil and sauce is ready to serve.

Makes about 4 cups (1 L)

1 can (28 ounces/796 mL) whole San Marzano tomatoes
¼ cup (60 mL) extra-virgin olive oil
6 cloves garlic, peeled and thinly sliced
Pinch of red pepper flakes
1 teaspoon (5 mL) kosher salt
1 teaspoon (5 mL) granulated sugar
2 large basil sprigs, with stems

Leave it to the potato-loving Crawford to dream up a soup inspired by colcannon, a traditional dish of mashed potatoes, bacon and cabbage. This hearty soup warms and comforts instantly on a cold winter night.

COLCANNON SOUP

Serves 4

4 slices slab bacon (each ½-inch/1 cm thick)
2 tablespoons (30 mL) unsalted butter
1 leek, white and light green parts only, halved lengthwise and thinly sliced crosswise
1 medium yellow onion, halved and thinly sliced crosswise
2 cloves garlic, minced
5 cups (1.25 L) cored and chopped savoy cabbage
½ cup (125 mL) dry white wine
4 cups (1 L) peeled and diced Yukon Gold potatoes
3 sprigs thyme
4 cups (1 L) chicken stock
2 cups (500 mL) heavy (35%) cream
Kosher salt and cracked black pepper
1 green onion, sliced on the diagonal

1. In a large pot over medium heat, cook bacon until crispy, about 5 minutes. With a slotted spoon, transfer bacon to paper towel to drain.

2. Drain bacon fat from skillet, then add butter and let it melt. Add leek, onion and garlic and cook until leek and onion are translucent, about 5 minutes, stirring frequently. Add cabbage and cook for 8 to 10 minutes, tossing frequently. Add wine and cook 2 minutes more.

3. Add potatoes, thyme, stock and cream. Bring to a boil, then reduce heat to medium-low and simmer until potatoes are tender and cabbage is soft, about 40 minutes more.

4. Remove thyme stems and season soup to taste with salt and pepper. Serve immediately, sprinkled with reserved bacon and green onions.

Kimchi is a spicy, earthy-flavoured dish of fermented vegetables that is eaten at breakfast, lunch and dinner in Korea. In traditional recipes, it is left to ferment for weeks, months or even years. My version—using cabbage, ginger, apple, chilies and green onions in a soy sauce brine—is ready the next day!

QUICK KIMCHI

1. Halve cabbage lengthwise and cut out the core. Cut cabbage into 1-inch (2.5 cm) chunks. You should have about 10 cups (2.5 L).

2. In a large pot of boiling salted water, blanch cabbage for 1 minute. Drain and transfer to a bowl of ice water to stop the cooking. Drain well, place in a large bowl and add carrot and apple. Set aside.

3. In a small saucepan over medium heat, bring vinegar, sugar and salt to a simmer and cook until sugar dissolves. Add garlic, green onions, chili and ginger and cook 1 minute more.

4. Pour vinegar mixture over cabbage mixture. Add cilantro, soy sauce and sesame oil and fold gently to combine.

5. Spoon kimchi into a 1-quart (1 L) mason jar, seal and refrigerate overnight to allow flavours to meld.

Makes about 4 cups (1 L)

1 napa cabbage
1 small carrot, peeled and thinly
    sliced on the diagonal
1 red Gala apple, peeled, cored and
    julienned
1 cup (250 mL) seasoned rice vinegar
2 tablespoons (30 mL) granulated
    sugar
1 teaspoon (5 mL) kosher salt
4 large cloves garlic, coarsely chopped
3 green onions, cut into 1-inch
    (2.5 cm) pieces
½ Fresno chili, sliced crosswise into
    thin rounds
5 thin slices peeled fresh ginger
½ cup (125 mL) coarsely chopped
    cilantro
3 tablespoons (45 mL) soy sauce
1 teaspoon (5 mL) sesame oil

GARLIC

I can't imagine a world without garlic. A little of it goes a long way, and the flavour of garlic changes depending on the variety and how you use it. When raw, garlic has a very strong and intoxicating, spicy flavour. When cooked, it can be mild, sweet and rich. Garlic's pungent taste makes it a flavour enhancer, and I love it prepared in a number of ways: lobster dipped in a pool of lemony garlic butter; hand-cut, crispy fries served with a side of aïoli; chicken baked with 40 cloves; or a thick slice of grilled crusty bread rubbed with roasted garlic and finished with sea salt. And then there are the recipes I share with you here. Without garlic, I simply would not care to cook!

Raw garlic has a strong, spicy flavour, but roasting enhances its flavour and adds a delicate sweetness, depth and richness. Roasted garlic is delicious on its own, but it will make just about any dish taste better. I always have a jar of roasted garlic in my fridge, both at home and at Ruby Watchco.

WHOLE ROASTED GARLIC

1. Preheat oven to 375°F (190°C) and line a 9-inch (23 cm) square baking pan with parchment paper.

2. Peel off and discard the papery outer layers of the garlic heads. Cut off the top third of each head to expose individual cloves. Place bulbs cut side up in baking pan. Arrange thyme and rosemary on top. Drizzle with oil and sprinkle with salt.

3. Cover pan with foil and bake bulbs until golden brown and cloves are very soft, about 1 hour.

4. Transfer pan to a wire rack, remove foil and discard thyme and rosemary. Let bulbs cool to room temperature. (Roasted garlic keeps, covered with foil and refrigerated, up to 3 days or can be frozen.)

Makes 8 heads

8 large heads garlic
6 sprigs thyme
2 sprigs rosemary
¼ cup (60 mL) extra-virgin olive oil
½ teaspoon (2 mL) kosher salt

This is a classic recipe with the emphasis on taste. A creamy risotto with the sweet, caramelized flavour of roasted garlic is a wonderful accompaniment to the tender and moist squab, drizzled with a fragrant hit of pepper over a sweet glaze. Three words come to mind: creamy, rich and indulgent. This risotto is also perfect with roasted chicken, grilled vegetables or on its own.

ROASTED GARLIC RISOTTO with MAPLE and BLACK PEPPER GLAZED SQUAB

1. Preheat oven to 350°F (180°C).

Prepare the Maple and Black Pepper Glazed Squab

2. In an ovenproof skillet over medium heat, heat oil. Add squab halves skin side down and cook until skin is browned, about 3 minutes. Turn over and cook for 2 minutes more.

3. Turn squab over again and add rosemary, maple syrup, butter and black pepper. Continue to cook squab, basting often, until skin is glistening and internal temperature of thigh meat reaches 125°F (50°C) for medium-rare doneness, about 3 minutes more. Remove from heat and set aside.

Make the Roasted Garlic Risotto

4. Squeeze garlic cloves into a small bowl and mash with a fork. Set aside.

5. In a skillet over medium heat, melt 1 tablespoon (15 mL) butter. Add olive oil and onion and cook for 2 to 3 minutes, until onions have softened. Add rice and continue to cook for 2 minutes, stirring constantly. Stir in reserved roasted garlic and 1 cup (250 mL) hot stock and stir until stock is completely absorbed by rice.

6. Continue ladling stock into rice, 1 cup (250 mL) at a time and stirring until liquid is absorbed before adding more, until rice is al dente, 15 to 18 minutes, stirring constantly.

7. When risotto is almost done, reheat squab in oven for 2 to 3 minutes.

8. Remove risotto from heat. Stir in Parmesan and remaining 2 table-spoons (30 mL) butter until combined. Season to taste with salt and pepper. Serve squab on top of risotto.

Serves 2

Maple and Black Pepper Glazed Squab

1 tablespoon (15 mL) vegetable oil
1 squab (about 1 pound/450 g), rinsed with cold water and patted dry, halved lengthwise through the breastbone and backbone removed
2 sprigs rosemary
2 tablespoons (30 mL) pure maple syrup
1 tablespoon (15 mL) unsalted butter
1 teaspoon (5 mL) cracked black pepper

Roasted Garlic Risotto

2 heads Whole Roasted Garlic (page 107)
3 tablespoons (45 mL) cold unsalted butter, divided
2 tablespoons (30 mL) olive oil
1 small onion, finely diced
2 cups (500 mL) arborio rice
4 to 5 cups (1 to 1.25 L) hot chicken stock, divided
1 cup (250 mL) finely grated Parmesan cheese
Kosher salt and cracked black pepper

Spaghetti all'aglio e olio is an Italian classic, a perfect example of simple, delicious comfort food. The combination of fine olive oil, lots and lots of garlic, chili flakes, lemon, parsley and Parmesan is truly incredible. In 20 minutes, dinner is served!

SPAGHETTI with OLIVE OIL, GARLIC, CHILI and LEMON

Serves 4

1 pound (450 g) spaghetti
⅓ cup (75 mL) extra-virgin olive oil
¼ cup (125 mL) thinly sliced garlic
    (about 6 to 8 cloves)
½ teaspoon (2 mL) red pepper flakes
Juice of ½ lemon
3 tablespoons (45 mL) finely chopped
    flat-leaf parsley
½ cup (125 mL) grated Parmesan
    cheese

1. Cook spaghetti according to package directions until al dente.

2. Meanwhile, in a large skillet set over medium-high heat, heat olive oil. Add garlic and red pepper flakes and cook until garlic is golden, about 3 minutes, stirring constantly. Remove from heat and stir in lemon juice.

3. Drain pasta, then add to skillet. Toss well to combine. Serve immediately, sprinkled with parsley and Parmesan.

ONIONS

I love starting a dish with a pan of onions and butter—it's the perfect way to unlock an onion's secrets. The key is low and slow cooking, which will turn a regular onion darkly silken and rich. It is that unbelievable smell and taste that calls me back to the kitchen every time. Onions are endlessly versatile and indispensable in the kitchen because they always, always deliver in the flavour department. There are many varieties of onions, and each differs in size, strength and colour. They're enjoyed in an array of dishes—on top of a burger or fried into Crispy Onion Rings, in a Steak and Onion Pie or on an Onion Rosemary Focaccia, in a salsa or a soup. So pick up a bag of your favourite onion and start chopping, slicing and dicing.

This onion marmalade is a staple in my kitchen, both at home and at the restaurant. I love pairing it with crackers, country paté, a cheese course or even adding it to a sandwich. It does take a bit of time to make, but most of that time is spent closely watching the pot of sliced onions transform into caramelized, rich, oniony goodness.

ONION MARMALADE

1. In a large skillet over medium heat, heat oil. Add onions, bay leaves, thyme and salt and cook until onions are translucent, about 15 minutes, stirring often.

2. Stir in balsamic and red wine vinegars and continue cooking until liquid evaporates and onions are deeply caramelized, 40 to 50 minutes.

3. Cool onion mixture to room temperature. Remove thyme stems and bay leaves, then spoon marmalade into an airtight container, cover and refrigerate until ready to use. Marmalade keeps in the fridge for up to 2 weeks.

Makes about 1 cup (250 mL)

3 tablespoons (45 mL) extra-virgin olive oil
8 cups (2 L) sliced mixed onions, such as red, Vidalia and Spanish
2 bay leaves
1 sprig thyme
1 teaspoon (5 mL) kosher salt
¼ cup (60 mL) balsamic vinegar
¼ cup (60 mL) red wine vinegar

I love a good meat pie, so I thought I would entice you with this steak and onion pie with golden flaky pastry and a scrumptious meaty filling. With the weather getting colder, it's time to pull out all the stops and create the ultimate in comfort food.

STEAK and ONION PIE

Serves 6

2 pounds (900 g) stewing beef, trimmed and cut into 2-inch (5 cm) cubes
½ cup (125 mL) all-purpose flour
3 tablespoons (45 mL) canola oil, divided
3 tablespoons (45 mL) unsalted butter, divided
1½ cups (375 mL) red wine, divided
2 tablespoons (30 mL) olive oil
1 medium white onion, chopped
1 large yellow onion, chopped
2 shallots, halved lengthwise
2 bay leaves
2 sprigs thyme
1 sprig rosemary
2 cups (500 mL) beef stock
Kosher salt and cracked black pepper
3 cups (750 mL) peeled and blanched pearl onions
1 sheet (8 ounces/225 g) frozen puff pastry, thawed in fridge overnight
1 large egg, lightly beaten

1. Dust beef with flour. In a large skillet over medium heat, heat 2 tablespoons (30 mL) canola oil and 2 tablespoons (30 mL) butter. Working in batches if necessary, brown beef cubes on all sides, 15 to 20 minutes in all. Transfer browned beef to a bowl.

2. Add ¾ cup (175 mL) red wine and, using a wooden spoon, scrape up any brown bits stuck to bottom of skillet. Scrape deglazing liquid into bowl with beef.

3. In a Dutch oven over medium-low heat, heat olive oil. Add white and yellow onions and shallots and sauté until golden, 12 to 15 minutes, stirring often.

4. Add bay leaves, thyme, rosemary, the remaining ¾ cup (175 mL) red wine, stock and reserved beef and its juices (including deglazing liquid). Stir to combine, then season to taste with salt and pepper. Simmer, uncovered, over medium-low heat until beef is fork-tender, about 2 hours.

5. Meanwhile, in another skillet over medium heat, melt remaining 1 tablespoon (15 mL) butter with 1 tablespoon (15 mL) canola oil. Add pearl onions and cook until golden, about 5 minutes, stirring often. Remove from heat.

6. Preheat oven to 375°F (190°C).

7. Remove and discard bay leaves, thyme and rosemary sprigs from beef, and stir in pearl onions. Spoon mixture into a greased baking dish and let cool 15 minutes before laying chilled pastry sheet on top. Trim edges of pastry if needed, cut a vent hole in top of the pastry and brush surface with beaten egg.

8. Bake pie until heated through and pastry is golden, 25 to 30 minutes. Let rest 5 minutes before serving.

Everyone knows that I love bread—and I love making bread. The aroma of this focaccia baking in the oven drives me crazy, it's so intoxicating. The spongy softness and the incredible flavour of this bread are sure to impress, and you'll be surprised how easy it is to make.

ONION ROSEMARY FOCACCIA

1. In a large bowl, stir together water, yeast and sugar and let stand for 5 minutes. Stir in 1 cup (250 mL) flour and ¼ cup (60 mL) oil and let stand for another 5 minutes. Stir in remaining 1¾ cups (425 mL) flour and the salt and turn dough out onto a lightly floured surface. Knead until smooth, about 3 to 4 minutes. Transfer to an oiled bowl, cover with plastic wrap and let stand for 1½ to 2 hours.

2. Preheat oven to 450°F (230°C).

3. In a large skillet over medium heat, heat 2 tablespoons (30 mL) oil. Add onion and cook for about 10 minutes, stirring occasionally. Add garlic and cook for about 5 to 10 minutes more, until onions are well caramelized.

4. Oil a 13- × 9-inch (32 × 23 cm) rimmed baking sheet. Transfer dough to baking sheet and press it down so it reaches the edges. Dimple dough all over with your fingers and drizzle with remaining 2 tablespoons (30 mL) oil. Let dough rise for about 30 minutes.

5. Scatter onion mixture over dough, then sprinkle with rosemary. Bake for 20 minutes, until golden brown. Garnish with sea salt.

Makes one 13- × 9-inch (32 × 23 cm) focaccia

1¼ cups (300 mL) warm water

2 packets (¼ ounce/7 g each) active dry yeast

1 tablespoon (15 mL) granulated sugar

2¾ cups (675 mL) "00" fine wheat flour, divided, plus more for dusting

½ cup (125 mL) extra-virgin olive oil, divided

2 teaspoons (10 mL) kosher salt

1 large onion, thinly sliced

2 cloves garlic, thinly sliced

2 sprigs rosemary, leaves coarsely chopped

Maldon sea salt

It's been said that onion rings are the least popular item on a burger joint's menu—they rarely get the love they deserve. So that's why I will always order up the onion rings when it's burger night at home. These rings are sweet, crispy, crunchy and quick to make! This batter is also perfect for frying cauliflower, broccoli, zucchini sticks and even fish.

CRISPY ONION RINGS

Serves 4 to 6

1¾ cups (425 mL) all-purpose flour
½ cup (125 mL) cornstarch
2 tablespoons (30 mL) cornmeal
4 teaspoons (20 mL) baking powder
1 teaspoon (5 mL) chili powder
1 teaspoon (5 mL) dry mustard
1 tablespoon (15 mL) kosher salt, plus
    extra for garnish
½ teaspoon (2 mL) black pepper
12 ounces (355 mL) lager-style beer
2 large sweet onions, such as Vidalia
Vegetable oil, for deep-frying

1. In a large bowl, whisk together flour, cornstarch, cornmeal, baking powder, chili powder, dry mustard, salt and pepper. Add beer and stir until smooth.

2. Cut onions crosswise into ½-inch (1 cm) slices and separate into rings.

3. In a deep, heavy saucepan, heat 4 inches (10 cm) oil to 375°F (190°C).

4. Working in batches, dip onion rings into the batter. Tap off excess batter. Carefully drop onion rings into oil and cook for about 2 minutes, turning rings over, until golden brown. Remove onion rings with a slotted spoon and drain on paper towel. Season with salt.

PARSNIPS

Parsnips have a complex taste. After that first frost, their high starch content converts into sugar, making them sweeter than their more colourful cousin, the carrot. They are sweet, yes, but they also have an earthy, nutty, buttery taste. Everyone should try baking with parsnips to see how versatile they are. I recommend my favourite Parsnip Cake with Cream Cheese Frosting, a spin on Ruby Watchco's famous carrot cake. The parsnip's soft, fragrant, slightly sweet flesh also adds a warm, comforting element to sauces, stews, soups, casseroles and even pancakes. You can use parsnips as you would use your favourite root vegetables in a gratin, like my Parsnip and Gruyère Gratin, or a poutine, like my Parsnip Poutine with Duck and Mushroom Gravy. You're missing out if you don't give this distinctive root a taste.

The smell of this gratin baking in the oven is just so tempting! Parsnips, onions, thyme and cream covered in melted Gruyère—who could resist? A cheese that's made for melting, Gruyère's rustic, aromatic and assertive flavour pairs perfectly with the parsnips.

PARSNIP and GRUYÈRE GRATIN

1. Preheat oven to 350°F (180°C). Butter a 2-quart (2 L) baking dish and a large piece of parchment paper.

2. In a large bowl, mix together parsnips, shallots, garlic, thyme, salt, pepper, nutmeg, cream and half of the Gruyère until combined. Spoon mixture into baking dish. Place parchment paper buttered side down on top and cover dish with foil.

3. Bake until parsnips are tender, about 80 minutes. Remove foil and parchment and sprinkle remaining Gruyère over top. Bake until cheese is melted and golden, about 15 minutes more. Let cool for 5 minutes before serving.

Serves 8

2 pounds (900 g) parsnips, peeled and thinly sliced on the diagonal
2 shallots, thinly sliced crosswise into thin rings
2 cloves garlic, minced
1 teaspoon (5 mL) fresh thyme leaves
2 teaspoons (10 mL) kosher salt
1 teaspoon (5 mL) cracked black pepper
Pinch of freshly grated nutmeg
1½ cups (375 mL) heavy (35%) cream
4 ounces (115 g) Gruyère cheese, coarsely grated, divided

Ask anyone what is a truly Canadian dish and they will tell you, "Poutine"! When I lived in Montreal in my twenties, I swear I would find some sort of poutine on every menu. I created this version of poutine after a night out on the town reading some of those menus.

PARSNIP POUTINE with DUCK and MUSHROOM GRAVY

Serves 4

Roasted Duck

4 large whole duck legs (about
    3½ pounds/1.6 kg total), trimmed
    of excess fat
Kosher salt and cracked black pepper
1 carrot, peeled and finely diced
1 small onion, finely diced
2 cloves garlic, peeled and crushed
2 sprigs thyme
1 sprig rosemary
1 cup (250 mL) white wine, such as
    Riesling or Gewürztraminer
3 cups (750 mL) chicken stock

Mushroom Gravy

4 tablespoons (60 mL) unsalted
    butter, divided
2 cups (500 mL) sliced cremini
    mushrooms
2 tablespoons (30 mL) finely diced
    shallot
1 clove garlic, minced
2 tablespoons (30 mL) all-purpose flour
1 cup (250 mL) red wine
1¼ cups (300 mL) chicken stock
1 teaspoon (5 mL) fresh thyme leaves
1 tablespoon (15 mL) chopped
    flat-leaf parsley
Kosher salt and cracked black pepper

Parsnip Poutine

2 pounds (900 g) parsnips, peeled and
    cut lengthwise into 3-inch (8 cm)
    batons
2 tablespoons (30 mL) extra-virgin
    olive oil
½ teaspoon (2 mL) kosher salt
¼ teaspoon (1 mL) cracked black
    pepper
1 cup (250 mL) cheese curds
1 tablespoon (15 mL) chopped
    flat-leaf parsley

Prepare the Roasted Duck

1. Preheat oven to 375°F (190°C) and line a baking sheet with parchment paper.

2. Heat a large ovenproof skillet over medium heat. Season duck legs with salt and pepper. Place legs skin side down in pan and cook for 3 to 4 minutes. Discard excess fat. Turn the legs and add carrot, onion, garlic, thyme and rosemary. Continue to cook, stirring occasionally, until vegetables start to caramelize.

3. Turn duck legs once more. Add white wine and stock. Using a wooden spoon, scrape up any brown bits on the bottom of the skillet. Transfer to oven and cook for 35 to 45 minutes, until duck is tender and liquid is reduced.

4. Remove pan from oven (but don't turn off the oven) and transfer duck legs to a plate to cool. Remove thyme and rosemary stems and reserve braising liquid for gravy. Remove and discard duck skin and pick meat from bone. Set aside.

Make the Mushroom Gravy

5. In a large skillet over medium-high heat, melt 2 tablespoons (30 mL) butter. Add mushrooms and cook until tender and most of their liquid has evaporated, about 10 minutes, stirring often. Add shallots and garlic and continue cooking for 1 to 2 minutes more, until shallots are softened. Transfer mushroom mixture to a bowl.

6. In skillet, melt remaining 2 tablespoons (30 mL) butter. Stir in flour and cook for 1 minute, stirring constantly. Whisk in red wine and cook until reduced by half, stirring often. Add stock and any reserved duck braising liquid and cook until gravy is thick enough to coat the back of a spoon, about 10 minutes. Stir in reserved duck meat, mushroom mixture, thyme and parsley, and season to taste with salt and pepper. Keep warm.

Make the Parsnip Fries

7. Toss parsnips with oil, salt and pepper. Spread in a single layer on baking sheet and roast until tender and golden brown, about 15 minutes, turning occasionally.

Assemble Parsnip Poutine

8. Place parsnips on serving platter. Top with cheese curds and parsley. Ladle hot Mushroom Gravy over top and serve immediately.

I've replaced carrots with parsnips in this twist on Ruby Watchco's famous carrot cake. Once you taste this cream cheese frosting combined with the natural sweetness and spiciness of the parsnips, you may never go back to carrots!

PARSNIP CAKE with CREAM CHEESE FROSTING

Make the Parsnip Cake

1. Preheat oven to 350°F (180°C). Butter two 9-inch (23 cm) round cake pans, line each with a circle of buttered parchment paper and lightly dust with flour.

2. In a large bowl, sift together flour, baking powder, baking soda, cinnamon, salt and nutmeg. In another bowl, stir together parsnips, coconut, walnuts and raisins.

3. In a stand mixer fitted with the paddle attachment, beat together sugar and oil on low speed until blended. Increase speed to medium and add eggs 1 at a time, beating well after each addition.

4. On low speed, add flour mixture and mix just until blended. Fold in parsnip mixture by hand just until combined.

5. Divide batter between prepared pans. Tap pans on work surface several times to level batter. Bake cakes until a toothpick inserted into the centre comes out clean, about 50 minutes. Transfer pans to a wire rack and let cool for 15 minutes. Run a sharp knife around the edge of each cake to loosen it, then invert cakes onto racks. Peel off parchment and let cakes cool completely before frosting.

Make the Cream Cheese Frosting

6. While cakes are baking, start the frosting. In a stand mixer fitted with the paddle attachment, beat cream cheese on medium speed until smooth. Add butter and beat until blended. Add icing sugar and lemon juice and beat until fluffy, about 3 minutes.

Assemble the Cake

7. With a long serrated knife, halve cooled cakes horizontally to make 4 layers.

8. Place 1 cake layer cut side up on a cake plate. Using an offset spatula, spread a quarter of the Cream Cheese Frosting over top, spreading right to the edge. Carefully set the second cake layer smooth side up on top and spread with a quarter more Cream Cheese Frosting. Repeat with remaining 2 layers.

9. Sprinkle top with coconut and refrigerate cake for at least 1 hour. For optimal flavour, let cake rest at room temperature for 30 minutes before serving.

Serves 12

Parsnip Cake

2 cups (500 mL) all-purpose flour
2 teaspoons (10 mL) baking powder
2 teaspoons (10 mL) baking soda
2 teaspoons (10 mL) cinnamon
1 teaspoon (5 mL) kosher salt
½ teaspoon (2 mL) freshly grated nutmeg
3 cups (750 mL) grated peeled parsnips
1 cup (250 mL) sweetened flaked coconut
1 cup (250 mL) chopped walnuts
½ cup (125 mL) seedless golden raisins
2 cups (500 mL) granulated sugar
1 cup (250 mL) grapeseed oil
4 large eggs

Cream Cheese Frosting

2 packages (8 ounces/225 g each) cream cheese, at room temperature
½ cup (125 mL) unsalted butter, at room temperature
2 cups (500 mL) icing sugar, sifted
1 tablespoon (15 mL) lemon juice

To Finish

½ cup (125 mL) toasted sweetened flaked coconut

POTATOES

When we were growing up, my brother Allan and I loved making supper with our dad. We eagerly awaited his arrival, and after big hugs, we all set off to the kitchen. We always had potatoes, so we helped by peeling them. After years of wonderful family dinners (with potatoes as the side!), you can understand why potatoes represent comfort and warmth to me. They are a classic winter staple in our kitchen. They store incredibly well in a cool, dry, dark area, and can be prepared in so many ways—boiled or roasted; fried into classic French Fries and served with spicy Chipotle Aïoli; or whipped to perfection in my Braised Lamb Shanks with Pommes Purée.

You haven't had French fries until you've had homemade French fries. Salty, crunchy on the outside, fluffy on the inside, dipped in a simple aïoli. Heaven. I love serving up my Chipotle Aïoli with these fries, but it's equally amazing with my Twice-Baked Fully Loaded Sweet Potatoes (page 89) or Jerk Shrimp Tostadas with Minted Melon Salsa (page 298).

FRENCH FRIES with CHIPOTLE AÏOLI

Serves 4

Chipotle Aïoli
1 cup (250 mL) mayonnaise
2 tablespoons (30 mL) chipotle
  peppers in adobo sauce

French Fries
2 pounds (900 g) russet potatoes
  (about 3 large), peeled and cut into
  batons
Vegetable oil, for deep-frying
Kosher salt and cracked black pepper

Make the Chipotle Aïoli
1. Place mayonnaise and chipotle in a blender and purée. Set aside or spoon into an airtight container and refrigerate for up to 5 days.

Prepare the French Fries
2. Cover potatoes with cold water and let soak for 1 hour. Drain and pat dry.

3. In a large, deep saucepan, heat 4 inches (10 cm) oil to 325°F (160°C). Set a wire rack inside a baking sheet.

4. Working in batches, blanch-fry potatoes until barely tender and still pale, about 5 minutes. With a slotted spoon, transfer to wire rack to drain. Repeat with remaining potatoes.

5. Preheat oven to 325°F (160°C). Heat oil to 375°F (190°C).

6. Working in batches, deep-fry potatoes until crisp and golden, about 4 minutes. With a slotted spoon, transfer fries to wire rack to drain and keep warm in oven while frying remaining potatoes. Season fries with salt and pepper to taste and serve immediately with Chipotle Aïoli.

When you have leftover mashed potatoes from the night before, you can quickly transform them into these classic potato cakes for breakfast or brunch—I love serving them with over-easy eggs and bacon. But this dish is a great way to serve up potatoes for a surprising change at dinnertime too.

BOXTY POTATOES

1. Cut half of the potatoes into 1-inch (2.5 cm) cubes; set aside. Coarsely grate the remaining potatoes. In a sieve placed over a bowl, toss grated potatoes with 1 teaspoon (5 mL) salt. Set aside for 30 minutes.

2. Meanwhile, preheat oven to 325°F (160°C).

3. In a saucepan of boiling salted water, boil cubed potatoes until fork-tender, 10 to 15 minutes. Drain, transfer to a large bowl and mash with 2 tablespoons (30 mL) butter and ¼ cup (60 mL) milk. Set aside.

4. In a large skillet over medium heat, melt remaining 2 tablespoons (30 mL) butter. Add green onions and cook until tender, about 5 minutes, stirring often. Remove from heat.

5. With your hands, squeeze any excess liquid out of grated potatoes. Add to mashed potatoes along with remaining ¾ cup (175 mL) milk, green onions, chives, flour, remaining 1 teaspoon (5 mL) salt and pepper. Stir to combine, then shape mixture into 8 patties.

6. In the skillet, heat ⅛ inch (3 mm) oil over medium heat. Working in batches and adding more oil if necessary, fry patties until golden brown on both sides, about 5 minutes per side. Transfer cooked patties to a baking sheet and keep warm in oven. Serve warm with a dollop of sour cream.

Serves 8

2 pounds (900 g) Yukon Gold potatoes, peeled
2 teaspoons (10 mL) kosher salt, divided
4 tablespoons (60 mL) unsalted butter, melted, divided
1 cup (250 mL) milk, divided
1 bunch green onions, thinly sliced on the diagonal
¼ cup (60 mL) finely chopped chives
⅓ cup (75 mL) all-purpose flour
½ teaspoon (2 mL) cracked black pepper
Canola oil, for frying
Sour cream, for serving

Braised lamb shanks are pure comfort food. Cooked to perfection, the flavourful meat will fall off the bone and melt in your mouth, and to top it all off, they're served with a side of velvety potatoes. Please don't judge me for the amount of butter used in this recipe. Yes, two parts potato, one part butter. Don't gasp, just try it. You'll love it!

BRAISED LAMB SHANKS with POMMES PURÉE

Serves 4

Braised Lamb Shanks

2 tablespoons (30 mL) olive oil
4 large lamb shanks (12 ounces to
    1 pound/340 to 450 g each)
3 carrots, peeled and diced
4 ribs celery, diced
4 shallots, chopped
1 large onion, chopped
4 cloves garlic, minced
1 cup (250 mL) dry red wine
1 can (28 ounces/796 mL) whole
    peeled tomatoes, tomatoes
    quartered
4 cups (1 L) chicken stock
2 sprigs rosemary
2 sprigs thyme
2 bay leaves
2 tablespoons (30 mL) unsalted butter
2 tablespoons (30 mL) chopped
    flat-leaf parsley
Kosher salt and cracked black pepper

Pommes Purée

2 pounds (900 g) Yukon Gold potatoes,
    peeled
1 pound (450 g) cold unsalted butter,
    cut into small cubes
⅓ cup (75 mL) milk
Kosher salt

Prepare the Braised Lamb Shanks

1. Preheat oven to 325°F (160°C).

2. In a large Dutch oven, heat olive oil over medium heat. Add shanks, 2 at a time, and brown both sides, 10 to 12 minutes per batch. Transfer shanks to a large plate.

3. Add carrots, celery, shallots, onion and garlic to the pot and cook until vegetables are tender, 8 to 10 minutes. Pour in wine and bring to a boil, then reduce for 3 to 4 minutes. Using a wooden spoon, scrape up any brown bits on the bottom of the pot.

4. Add tomatoes with their juice, stock, rosemary, thyme and bay leaves. Return lamb shanks to pot, submerging them in the braising liquid. Bring to a boil, cover and place in the oven. Braise for 1½ to 2 hours, until the meat is nearly falling off the bone.

Make the Pommes Purée

5. While the lamb is braising, in a large pot, cover potatoes with cold salted water. Bring to a boil, then reduce heat to low and simmer for 35 to 40 minutes or until tender. Drain, transfer to a bowl and let potatoes cool slightly.

6. Push potatoes through a food mill on the finest setting and return to the pot. Stir over medium heat until potatoes are heated through. Add butter a few cubes at a time, allowing each addition to almost melt before adding the next, until it all has been incorporated.

7. Warm the milk in a small pot and add to potatoes. Using a whisk, vigorously stir potatoes until fluffy. Season to taste with salt. Cover and keep warm.

To Finish

8. Using tongs, remove shanks from the Dutch oven and place on a clean plate. Spoon off as much fat as possible from the surface of the braising liquid. Strain braising liquid into a small pot and reduce over medium heat until thickened slightly. Remove from heat and whisk in butter and parsley. Season to taste with salt and pepper.

9. Divide Pommes Purée among plates, place lamb shanks on top and spoon sauce over the meat.

RUTABAGA

This is another Crawford favourite, and not just once a year at a Robbie Burns supper. This is a vegetable you want to eat when you're craving a little soul or a friendly hug. Sometimes known as swedes, yellow turnips or, as my mother called them, neeps, rutabagas are treated the same as turnips. I recommend you use them like my mom, as an amazing topping for a shepherd's pie, because their flesh is a gorgeous buttery-yellow colour. (One of her Scottish chef tricks!) Rutabagas are best roasted, puréed or turned into rustic soups and stews. They can be enjoyed in the simplest way, like my Neeps and Butter, or in an exotically curry-spiced Punjabi dish, Butter Chicken with Rutabaga.

"Neeps" isn't a word you hear much in Canada—it's what the Scottish call rutabagas. This wonderful globe-shaped root was one of the first vegetables I learned how to cook. It's easy to peel with a sharp vegetable peeler, and whether roasted, baked or boiled and mashed with lots butter, it's the best! These neeps would be delicious alongside a few slices of honey baked ham.

NEEPS and BUTTER

1. Place rutabaga in a saucepan, cover with cold water and bring to a boil over high heat. Reduce heat to medium-low, cover and cook until fork-tender, about 15 minutes.

2. Drain rutabaga and return to saucepan. Add cream and 2 tablespoons (30 mL) butter and mash to combine. Season to taste with salt and pepper.

3. Spoon rutabaga purée into a serving bowl. Make a well in the centre with the back of the spoon and add remaining 2 tablespoons (30 mL) butter. Serve immediately.

Serves 4

1 rutabaga (about 2 pounds/900 g), peeled and cut into 1-inch (2.5 cm) cubes
¼ cup (60 mL) heavy (35%) cream
4 tablespoons (60 mL) unsalted butter, melted, divided
Kosher salt and cracked black pepper

Indian cooking is considered one of the most diverse cuisines in the world, and I am such a fan. Along with chicken tikka masala, butter chicken is without a doubt one of the most well-known dishes. I love its spices and bold flavours, and in my twist on the dish, the rutabaga is a wonderful addition to this classic. This one-pot wonder is guaranteed to impress.

BUTTER CHICKEN with RUTABAGA

Serves 4 to 6

Parsnip Chips
8 cups (2 L) vegetable oil
1 pound (450 g) parsnips
Kosher salt and cracked black pepper

Chicken and Marinade
1 cup (250 mL) plain Greek yogurt
3 tablespoons (45 mL) unsalted
    butter, melted
1 tablespoon (15 mL) lemon juice
1 tablespoon (15 mL) grated peeled
    fresh ginger
2 teaspoons (10 mL) minced garlic
1 tablespoon (15 mL) chili powder
1 tablespoon (15 mL) garam masala
½ teaspoon (2 mL) kosher salt
1½ pounds (675 g) boneless, skinless
    chicken breasts, cut into 1-inch
    (2.5 cm) cubes

Sauce
1 tablespoon (15 mL) unsalted butter
1 tablespoon (15 mL) canola oil
2 tablespoons (30 mL) garam masala
1 tablespoon (15 mL) minced garlic
1 tablespoon (15 mL) grated peeled
    fresh ginger
1 tablespoon (15 mL) seeded and
    minced hot green chili
1 tablespoon (15 mL) lemon juice
2 cups (500 mL) diced rutabaga
1 can (28 ounces/796 mL) crushed
    tomatoes
3 tablespoons (45 mL) honey
1 tablespoon (15 mL) chili powder
2 teaspoons (10 mL) dried crumbled
    fenugreek leaves
1 cup (250 mL) heavy (35%) cream
Kosher salt and cracked black pepper
6 cups (1.5 L) hot basmati rice, for
    serving
Chopped cilantro, for garnish

Make the Parsnip Chips

1. Heat vegetable oil in a large pot over high heat to 375°F (190°C). Set a wire rack inside a baking sheet. While oil heats, lay a parsnip flat on a cutting board, and using a vegetable peeler, peel off 4 to 5 wide noodle-shaped strips. Rotate parsnip 90 degrees and repeat. Continue to rotate until you can no longer peel any strips. Repeat with remaining parsnips.

2. Gently add a small handful of parsnips to the oil, stirring gently, and fry until lightly browned and crisp, 1 to 1½ minutes. Remove crisps from oil using a spider or slotted spoon; hold over the pot and allow to drain for 30 seconds. Transfer to wire rack and sprinkle with salt and pepper. Repeat with remaining parsnips, heating oil to 375°F (190°C) between batches. Once completely cooled, you can store the chips in an airtight container for up to 3 days.

Marinate and Bake the Chicken

3. In a large bowl, stir together yogurt, butter, lemon juice, ginger, garlic, chili powder, garam masala and salt until combined. Add chicken and toss to coat. Cover and refrigerate for 2 hours.

4. Preheat oven to 400°F (200°C). Line a baking sheet with foil and coat lightly with cooking spray.

5. Spread marinated chicken in a single layer on baking sheet and bake until cooked through, about 20 minutes.

Make the Sauce

6. While chicken is baking, in a large saucepan over medium heat, melt butter. Add oil and garam masala and stir-fry 1 minute. Add garlic, ginger, green chili, lemon juice and rutabaga and cook for 5 minutes, stirring occasionally.

7. Stir in crushed tomatoes, honey, chili powder and fenugreek. Bring to a boil, then reduce heat to low. Stir in cream, cover and simmer until rutabaga is tender, about 45 minutes, stirring occasionally.

8. Fold cooked chicken and any accumulated juices into sauce and cook until chicken is thoroughly heated, about 15 minutes, stirring occasionally. Season to taste with salt and pepper.

9. To serve, ladle chicken over basmati rice. Garnish with cilantro and Parsnip Chips and serve immediately.

SQUASH

It's the great pumpkin that seems to get most of the attention in late fall, but the many other varieties of squash that are harvested at the same time are the ones that you will keep on cooking throughout the colder months. From acorn, buttercup and delicata to Hubbard, spaghetti and kabocha, each variety has its own beautiful appearance, size, shape, delicious flavour and characteristic texture. If you're not familiar with all of these, I recommend you explore your local farmers' market and take home a few new varieties. Head into your kitchen, split one open and marvel at its gorgeous colour and aroma. Now it's time to enjoy the best part, transforming these beautiful centrepieces into delicious dishes that are the stars of cold-weather cooking.

Sometimes simple really is best. This is exactly how we served butternut squash when I was growing up, roasted with a touch of sweet maple syrup, brown sugar and warm spices to bring it all together. As a bonus, your kitchen will smell amazing as the squash cooks!

WHOLE ROASTED BUTTERNUT SQUASH with MAPLE SYRUP and BROWN SUGAR

1. Preheat oven to 450°F (230°C).

2. Cut squash in half and discard seeds. Place cut side up in a shallow baking dish. Divide butter, maple syrup and brown sugar between the two cavities. Sprinkle both halves with chili powder, cinnamon, and salt and pepper.

3. Roast for 45 to 50 minutes, or until flesh is fork-tender. Remove from oven and allow to cool slightly. Scoop flesh into a large bowl and mash together well with a spoon. Serve hot.

Serves 4 to 6

1 large butternut squash (about 1½ pounds/675 g)
¼ cup (60 mL) unsalted butter
¼ cup (60 mL) pure maple syrup
¼ cup (60 mL) light brown sugar
2 teaspoons (10 mL) chili powder
½ teaspoon (2 mL) cinnamon
Kosher salt and cracked black pepper

The comforting flavours of maple and sage pair perfectly with roasted squash and apples. And then there's the cheddar, which takes on a whole new personality in the crispy, cheesy garnish that's the star of the dish.

APPLE CIDER ROASTED SQUASH with SPICY WALNUTS and CHEDDAR FRICO

Serves 4 to 6

2 acorn squashes, halved, seeded and cut into ½-inch (1 cm) wedges
3 medium apples, such as Gala or Cortland, cored and cut into ½-inch (1 cm) slices (about 3 cups/750 mL)
½ cup (125 mL) dark brown sugar
¼ cup (60 mL) unsalted butter, melted
2 tablespoons (30 mL) olive oil
¼ cup (60 mL) pressed sweet apple cider
8 tablespoons (120 mL) pure maple syrup, divided
¼ teaspoon (1 mL) grated nutmeg
2 sprigs sage, leaves only
2 sprigs rosemary
Kosher salt and cracked black pepper
1 cup (250 mL) toasted walnut halves
½ teaspoon (2 mL) Espelette pepper
½ to 1 teaspoon (2 to 5 mL) Maldon sea salt
1 cup (250 mL) grated aged cheddar cheese

1. Preheat oven to 350°F (180°C).

2. In a large bowl, combine squash, apples, brown sugar, butter, olive oil, apple cider, 2 tablespoons (30 mL) maple syrup, nutmeg, sage and rosemary; toss together. Season with salt and pepper. Transfer to a roasting pan and bake for 45 minutes, stirring once. Remove the rosemary sprigs.

3. Meanwhile, combine walnut halves, remaining 6 tablespoons (90 mL) maple syrup and Espelette pepper in a small nonstick skillet. Bring to a boil, stirring frequently. Reduce heat and cook for 3 to 4 minutes or until the maple syrup has reduced to a thick glaze coating the pecans. Spread out on a baking sheet and sprinkle with sea salt.

4. Heat an 8-inch (20 cm) nonstick pan over medium-high heat. Spread ¼ cup (60 mL) cheddar into a 4-inch circle. Cook until cheese is light brown on the bottom. Turn over with a plastic spatula and continue cooking for another 10 to 15 seconds. Remove to a plate to cool. Wipe pan and repeat to make 4 fricos.

5. Spoon butternut squash into a serving dish and top with maple-glazed walnuts and cheddar fricos. Serve immediately.

Wild rice is not rice at all. It's an incredible aquatic grass that is extremely difficult to harvest. Its subtly nutty flavour combines so well with the squash in this winter salad. An added bonus: it's delicious served hot or cold.

BUTTERNUT SQUASH and WILD RICE SALAD with PUMPKIN SEED VINAIGRETTE

1. In a fine-mesh sieve, rinse wild rice under cold running water. Shake to drain. Transfer to a saucepan and add the water and salt. Bring to a boil, then reduce heat to a simmer. Cover and simmer for 45 minutes. Rice should be chewy and some grains will have burst open. It may need an additional 10 to 15 minutes. Keep checking the rice until the grains are tender.

2. When rice is done, pour it into a strainer to drain off any remaining liquid. Fluff rice with a fork and set aside.

3. In a skillet over medium heat, heat oil. Add squash and thyme and cook until squash is golden, about 15 minutes, stirring often.

4. Add butter and shallots and cook until shallots are translucent, about 3 minutes. Add chili powder and raisins and cook for 1 minute more. Add vinegar and pumpkin seed oil. Using a wooden spoon, scrape up any browned bits stuck to the bottom of skillet.

5. Fold in 3 cups (750 mL) rice and pumpkin seeds and cook until thoroughly heated. Season to taste with salt and pepper, then toss gently with parsley and kale. Serve immediately.

Serves 6

1 cup (250 mL) wild rice
5 cups (1.25 L) water
1 teaspoon (5 mL) salt
2 tablespoons (30 mL) olive oil
2 cups (500 mL) peeled, seeded and diced butternut squash
1 teaspoon (5 mL) fresh thyme leaves
2 tablespoons (30 mL) unsalted butter
¼ cup (60 mL) julienned shallots
1 teaspoon (5 mL) chili powder
½ cup (125 mL) seedless sultana raisins
¼ cup (60 mL) sherry vinegar
2 tablespoons (30 mL) pumpkin seed oil
½ cup (125 mL) toasted pumpkin seeds
Kosher salt and cracked black pepper
¼ cup (60 mL) flat-leaf parsley leaves
¼ cup (60 mL) baby kale

I love to see the look on people's faces the first time they cook with spaghetti squash. The unique spaghetti-like texture of the flesh makes this a healthy replacement in any recipe that calls for spaghetti—it's flavourful and satisfying, lighter and lower in carbs than pasta. I need to thank Chef Lora for this recipe. The combo of squash and a hazelnut cream sauce is simply brilliant. This is a fantastic accompaniment to roast chicken, pan-seared salmon or halibut.

SPAGHETTI SQUASH in HAZELNUT CREAM

Serves 4 to 6

1 spaghetti squash
¼ cup (60 mL) extra-virgin olive oil
Kosher salt and cracked black pepper
2 tablespoons (30 mL) unsalted butter
1 shallot, minced
1 clove garlic, minced
1 teaspoon (5 mL) fresh thyme leaves
½ cup (125 mL) dry white wine
1½ cups (375 mL) heavy (35%) cream
⅔ cup (150 mL) toasted hazelnuts,
    finely chopped, divided

1. Preheat oven to 450°F (230°C) and line a baking sheet with foil.

2. Split squash in half and scrape out seeds. Brush cut sides with olive oil, then season with salt and pepper. Place cut side down on baking sheet and roast for 30 to 40 minutes, until fork-tender. Remove from oven and let rest until cool enough to handle.

3. When squash is cool enough to handle, use a large kitchen spoon to scrape the strands of squash from the inside of the skin.

4. Melt butter in a medium saucepan over medium-high heat. Add shallot and garlic and sauté for 3 to 4 minutes, until shallots are softened. Add thyme and continue to sauté for an additional minute. Add wine and simmer until the pan is almost dry. Stir in cream and half the hazelnuts. Simmer until cream has reduced by half, 5 to 6 minutes. Season with salt and pepper.

5. Add squash and toss gently. Garnish with remaining hazelnuts and serve immediately.

Elegant and light, this mousse brings out the familiar flavours of traditional pumpkin pie layered between sweet, crisp brown sugar meringue wafers.

WHITE CHOCOLATE PUMPKIN MOUSSE with BROWN SUGAR MERINGUES

Make the Brown Sugar Meringues

1. Arrange racks in top and bottom thirds of oven. Preheat oven to 250°F (120°C). Line 2 baking sheets with parchment paper. On each paper, draw 4 rectangles, each 4 × 2 inches (10 × 5 cm). Turn paper over.

2. In a large bowl, beat egg whites and vanilla with a mixer at high speed until foamy. Gradually add sugar, beating until stiff peaks form.

3. Divide meringue evenly among the 8 rectangles. Using the back of a spoon, shape meringues into wafers with sides 1 inch (2.5 cm) high. Bake for 1 hour, rotating baking sheets top to bottom and front to back after 30 minutes. Turn oven off and let meringues cool in closed oven for 2 hours. Remove from oven and set aside. Once completely cooled, you can store the meringues in an airtight container for up to 1 week.

Make the White Chocolate Pumpkin Mousse

4. When meringues are cool, in a large bowl, beat together cream, vanilla and salt until stiff peaks form.

5. In another large bowl, beat egg whites with cleaned beaters until soft peaks form. Gradually add sugar and continue beating until stiff peaks form. Gently fold in chocolate, pumpkin purée, cinnamon and nutmeg.

6. Gently fold whipped cream into egg white mixture until completely incorporated.

Assemble the Dessert

7. Place 1 meringue on each plate, then spoon White Chocolate Pumpkin Mousse on top. Place another meringue on top and dust with icing sugar. Serve immediately.

Serves 4

Brown Sugar Meringues

1½ cups (375 mL) egg whites (from about 12 large eggs)
1 tablespoon (15 mL) pure vanilla extract
3 cups (750 mL) dark brown sugar

White Chocolate Pumpkin Mousse

1⅔ cups (400 mL) heavy (35%) cream
2 teaspoons (10 mL) pure vanilla extract
½ teaspoon (2 mL) salt
4 large egg whites, at room temperature
½ cup (125 mL) granulated sugar
4 ounces (115 g) chopped white chocolate, melted and cooled
½ cup (125 mL) pumpkin purée
½ teaspoon (2 mL) cinnamon
Pinch of nutmeg

To Serve

Icing sugar, for dusting

This is my go-to drink when the weather gets cold. This sweet, spicy espresso with notes of pumpkin, cinnamon, nutmeg and chocolate takes the chill out of a cold winter day and is such a treat!

SPICED PUMPKIN LATTES

Serves 4

¾ cup (175 mL) heavy (35%) cream
3 tablespoons (45 mL) granulated
    sugar
3 cups (750 mL) 2% milk
8 ounces (225 g) good-quality white
    chocolate, chopped
1 cup (250 mL) pumpkin purée
1 teaspoon (5 mL) pure vanilla extract
Demerara sugar, for the rim
1 teaspoon (5 mL) pumpkin pie spice
1 tablespoon (15 mL) unsalted butter,
    melted
4 shots espresso

1. Beat cream and sugar in a medium bowl until stiff peaks form. Cover and refrigerate whipped cream until ready to serve.

2. In a large, heavy saucepan over medium-high heat, bring milk to a simmer. Add white chocolate, pumpkin purée and vanilla. Whisk until melted and smooth. Return to a simmer, whisking constantly. Remove from heat.

3. Stir together Demerara sugar and pumpkin pie spice and pour onto a small plate. Brush the rims of 4 mugs with melted butter and dip into the spiced sugar.

4. Ladle pumpkin hot chocolate into mugs. Add a shot of espresso to each mug and top with dollops of whipped cream. Serve immediately.

SUNCHOKES

Sunchokes, also known as Jerusalem artichokes, are little brown knobby tubers (which from a distance look like ginger) from a variety of sunflower plant that is indigenous to North America. There's increasing interest in these golden nuggets, and you will see them popping up more and more at your local farmers' market. They are a real underground treasure—earthy in taste, even a bit smoky, and hugely versatile. Pickled and thinly sliced, they add a nutty taste and crunchy texture to my Warm Winter Sunchoke Salad. They are delicious all crisped up and browned in butter with garlic and rosemary, and their flesh becomes fluffy and sweet when roasted whole in salt. I think they make the best-tasting Sunchoke Soup, where they provide a wonderful velvety texture and light smoky flavour.

This spectacular dish is a must-try. I'm always amazed at how simple and delicious some recipes can be, and this one is super-high on the list! I love to gild these sweet, nutty, spicy nuggets with a generous hit of grated Parmesan just before serving.

SAUTÉED SUNCHOKES with CHILIES, HONEY and CUMIN

1. In a large skillet over medium-high heat, heat oil. Add sunchokes and brown on all sides, about 5 minutes.

2. Add garlic, chili, honey and cumin and cook for 3 minutes, stirring frequently.

3. Stir in vinegar and cook until liquid is absorbed and sunchokes are nicely glazed, about 3 minutes more, then season with salt and pepper. Garnish with parsley, if using, and serve immediately.

Serves 4

1 tablespoon (15 mL) extra-virgin olive oil
1 pound (450 g) sunchokes, scrubbed and quartered lengthwise
2 cloves roasted garlic (page 107), mashed into a paste
2 tablespoons (30 mL) thinly sliced Fresno chili rings
1 tablespoon (15 mL) honey
½ teaspoon (2 mL) ground cumin
2 tablespoons (30 mL) apple cider vinegar
Kosher salt and cracked black pepper
Chopped flat-leaf parsley, for garnish, if desired

These sunchoke chips are especially delicious when served up in a big bowl right alongside this flavourful sunchoke and white bean hummus. This creamy dip is always ready to tame your "chip and dip" cravings!

SUNCHOKE CHIPS and ROASTED SUNCHOKE HUMMUS

Serves 4 to 6

Roasted Sunchoke Hummus

½ pound (225 g) sunchokes, scrubbed
  and chopped
¼ cup (60 mL) plus 2 tablespoons
  (30 mL) olive oil
Kosher salt and cracked black pepper
1 cup (250 mL) drained and rinsed
  canned cannellini beans
1 head Whole Roasted Garlic
  (page 107), cloves squeezed out
Juice of 1 lemon

Sunchoke Chips

1 pound (450 g) sunchokes, scrubbed
  and patted dry
Vegetable oil, for deep-frying
Kosher salt

To Serve

Grated lemon zest

Make the Roasted Sunchoke Hummus

1. Preheat oven to 400°F (200°C) and line a baking sheet with parchment paper.

2. Toss sunchokes with 2 tablespoons (30 mL) olive oil, salt and pepper. Spread them evenly on the baking sheet and roast, stirring once, for 25 minutes, or until tender.

3. Let sunchokes cool slightly before transferring them to a food processor. Pulse-chop into a rough paste. Add beans and garlic. With processor running, slowly pour in lemon juice and remaining ¼ cup (60 mL) olive oil, processing until blended. Season to taste with salt and pepper. Scrape into a serving bowl, cover and refrigerate until ready to serve.

Make the Sunchoke Chips

4. Using a mandoline or vegetable peeler, slice sunchokes into paper-thin rounds.

5. In a medium, deep saucepan, heat 4 inches (10 cm) oil to 375°F (190°C).

6. Working in batches, add sunchoke rounds 1 at a time to hot oil and fry until crisp and golden, about 3 minutes. With a slotted spoon, transfer chips to paper towel to drain and season lightly with salt. Repeat with remaining sunchokes.

7. Garnish Roasted Sunchoke Hummus with lemon zest and more black pepper. Serve with Sunchoke Chips alongside.

This velvety soup highlights the smoky, earthy flavour of sunchokes. Each time I make this soup, I'm still surprised how magical these little tubers are—they are packed with flavour. Also named the "Canadian truffle", and just like that prized ingredient, a little goes a long way!

SUNCHOKE SOUP

1. In a large saucepot over medium heat, heat oil and butter. Add onion and garlic and cook until onion has softened, about 5 minutes, stirring often.

2. Add the sunchokes, potato, lemon zest, thyme and stock. Cook until potato is fork tender, about 20 to 25 minutes.

3. Remove thyme stems and purée soup with an immersion blender. Stir in cream and season to taste with salt and pepper. Serve hot, garnished with sunchoke chips, herbs and seedlings, if using.

Serves 4

2 tablespoons (30 mL) extra-virgin olive oil
1 tablespoon (15 mL) unsalted butter
1 small yellow onion, chopped
2 cloves garlic, chopped
1 pound (450 g) sunchokes, peeled and thinly sliced
1 large russet potato, peeled and diced
Grated zest of ½ lemon
2 sprigs thyme
4 cups (1 L) chicken stock
¼ cup (60 mL) heavy (35%) cream
Kosher salt and cracked black pepper
Sunchoke Chips (see page 154), for garnish, if desired
Fresh herbs or seedlings, for garnish, if desired

A good salad has a variety of tasty ingredients. A great salad, however, has that and a combination of interesting textures. Bitter greens, smoked bacon, earthy chanterelles and crunchy, tart sunchoke pickles tossed together with a citrusy-sweet warm date vinaigrette . . . What could be better than that?

WARM WINTER SUNCHOKE SALAD

1. Place frisée and pickled sunchokes in a large bowl.

2. In a skillet over medium heat, fry bacon until crispy. Transfer bacon to paper towel to drain. Remove all but 2 tablespoons (30 mL) bacon fat from skillet. Add chanterelles and shallot and cook until chanterelles are golden and their liquid has evaporated. Stir in dates, orange zest and juice, orange segments and vinegar and cook until warmed through. Season to taste with salt and pepper

3. Spoon warm vinaigrette over frisée mixture along with reserved bacon. Toss to combine and serve immediately.

Serves 4

Leaves from 1 head frisée
½ cup (125 mL) drained Pickled
   Sunchokes (see below)
4 slices bacon, chopped
1 cup (250 mL) quartered
   chanterelle mushrooms
1 tablespoon (15 mL) minced shallot
½ cup (125 mL) chopped pitted dates
Grated zest and juice of 1 orange
1 orange, peeled and cut into
   segments
3 tablespoons (45 mL) sherry vinegar
Kosher salt and cracked black pepper

This pickle recipe really makes sunchokes shine. The turmeric lends its brilliant yellow colour, making them wonderful to look at, but better to eat!

PICKLED SUNCHOKES

1. Place sunchokes in a 2-cup (500 mL) airtight container.

2. In a saucepan over medium heat, bring vinegar, water, sugar, ginger, garlic, shallot, chili rings, red pepper flakes, turmeric and salt to a boil, then reduce heat to medium-low and simmer until sugar dissolves.

3. Pour hot vinegar mixture over sunchokes and let cool to room temperature. Seal and refrigerate overnight to allow flavours to meld. These will keep in the refrigerator for up to 1 month.

Makes about 2 cups (500 mL)

1 pound (450 g) sunchokes, peeled
   and thinly sliced crosswise
1 cup (250 mL) seasoned rice vinegar
1 cup (250 mL) water
⅓ cup (75 mL) granulated sugar
4 thin slices peeled fresh ginger
2 cloves garlic, thinly sliced
1 small shallot, thinly sliced crosswise
   and separated into rings
1 tablespoon (15 mL) thinly sliced
   Fresno chili rings
½ teaspoon (2 mL) red pepper flakes
½ teaspoon (2 mL) turmeric
½ teaspoon (2 mL) kosher salt

TURNIPS

Turnips are ancient little treasures that are often ignored, but really, they've stood the test of time. They are a member of the mustard family and have an absolutely wonderful peppery bite that softens when they are cooked. Baby turnips are just as amazing. You don't have to peel these tender, spicy vegetables: just cut them into wedges and enjoy their crunch and zippy taste in a salad or vegetable platter. They make the perfect pickle and love all spices, which I'll show you in my Mustard-Spiced Pickled Turnips. They are also my go-to vegetable for a quick and tasty stir-fry, as in my Brown Butter Turnips with Sweet-and-Sour Turnip Greens.

For those of you not yet won over by turnips, let me introduce to you the secret ingredient that will change your mind: brown butter! Cooking the baby turnips first brings out their natural sweetness. A quick finish in nutty brown butter and a touch of savoury soy sauce seals the deal. These are excellent served alongside the Juniper-Roasted Venison Loin with Turnip Purée, as pictured on page 165.

BROWN BUTTER TURNIPS with SWEET-AND-SOUR TURNIP GREENS

1. In a skillet over medium heat, heat oil. Add turnips and cook until golden, about 15 minutes, stirring often.

2. Add butter, garlic, thyme, sugar and red pepper flakes. Cook 1 minute more, then add vinegar and cook until liquid has been absorbed. Add soy sauce, reduce heat to medium-low and continue cooking until turnips are tender, about 5 minutes more. Discard thyme stems. Transfer turnips to a plate.

3. Increase skillet heat to medium-high, and to pan juices add turnip greens and sesame seeds. Sauté until greens are barely wilted, about 1 minute, tossing continuously.

4. Return turnips to skillet and cook until nicely glazed, about 2 minutes more, then season with salt and pepper. Serve immediately.

Serves 4 to 6

2 tablespoons (30 mL) olive oil
2 cups (500 mL) peeled and quartered baby turnips
1 tablespoon (15 mL) unsalted butter
1 clove garlic, minced
2 sprigs thyme
1 tablespoon (15 mL) granulated sugar
¼ teaspoon (1 mL) red pepper flakes
2 teaspoons (10 mL) seasoned rice vinegar
2 teaspoons (10 mL) soy sauce
2 cups (500 mL) chopped turnip greens
¼ cup (60 mL) toasted sesame seeds
Kosher salt and cracked black pepper

There is so much going on in this pickle recipe. I love when intense flavours are combined to give your taste buds a real wake-up call. Dates, mustard, garlic, chili, sugar and apple cider vinegar all come together in this explosive pickle paste. Not only for turnips, you can use the pickling base on any of your favourite fall vegetables or fruits.

MUSTARD-SPICED PICKLED TURNIPS

1. Preheat oven to 400°F (200°C) and line a baking sheet with parchment paper.

2. Toss baby turnips in mustard oil, salt and pepper. Spread in a single layer on a baking sheet and roast for 10 to 15 minutes or until soft on the inside and slightly caramelized outside.

3. Meanwhile, in a medium saucepan over medium heat, cook vinegar and sugar until sugar dissolves. Stir in dates, raisins, garlic, mustard seeds, chili powder, peppercorns and cumin. Cook until dates break down and mixture thickens, about 20 minutes, stirring often.

4. Season date mixture to taste with salt and pepper, then stir in reserved turnips until well coated. Heat thoroughly. Spoon into a serving bowl and serve immediately or serve at room temperature. Turnips can be stored in the refrigerator in a sealed jar for up to 1 week.

Serves 4

1 pound (450 g) baby turnips, peeled and quartered
2 tablespoons (30 mL) mustard oil
Kosher salt and cracked black pepper
½ cup (125 mL) apple cider vinegar
¼ cup (60 mL) granulated sugar
6 pitted dates, finely chopped
½ cup (125 mL) seedless golden raisins
2 cloves garlic, minced
2 teaspoons (10 mL) yellow mustard seeds
2 teaspoons (10 mL) chili powder
1 teaspoon (5 mL) black peppercorns
½ teaspoon (2 mL) ground cumin

This recipe is a cottage favourite when the weather turns cold. The spicy, aromatic dark juniper berries are the perfect complement to the rustic, gamey flavour of venison. I'd highly recommend serving my Brown Butter Turnips with Sweet-and-Sour Turnip Greens (page 161) alongside these perfectly cooked, well-seasoned venison medallions and silky, creamy turnip purée.

JUNIPER-ROASTED VENISON LOIN with TURNIP PURÉE

Serves 4

Turnip Purée

1 pound (450 g) turnips, peeled and
    diced
2 cups (500 mL) whole milk
1 cup (250 mL) water
Kosher salt
½ to ¾ cup (125 to 175 mL) heavy
    (35%) cream
3 tablespoons (45 mL) unsalted butter
Kosher salt and cracked black pepper

Juniper-Roasted Venison Loin

1 venison loin (12 to 14 ounces/340 to
    400 g)
Kosher salt and cracked black pepper
1 tablespoon (15 mL) olive oil
3 tablespoons (45 mL) unsalted butter
1 teaspoon (5 mL) crushed juniper
    berries
1 clove garlic, crushed
2 sprigs thyme

Make the Turnip Purée

1. In a large saucepan, combine turnips, milk, water and a pinch of salt. Bring to a boil, then reduce heat and simmer for 20 minutes, or until turnips are very soft.

2. Drain turnips and transfer to a blender. Add ½ cup (125 mL) cream and the butter, and purée until smooth, adding more cream if necessary. Season with salt and pepper and keep warm until ready to serve

Prepare the Juniper-Roasted Venison Loin

3. Preheat oven to 350°F (180°C).

4. Season venison loin with salt and pepper. Heat oil in an ovenproof sauté pan over medium-high heat. Sear loin on all sides, about 2 minutes. Add butter, crushed juniper berries, garlic and thyme. Baste loin with butter, then transfer to oven.

5. Roast for 3 to 4 minutes, then turn loin and continue cooking for 2 to 3 minutes, until internal temperature in the thickest part of the loin reaches 130 to 135°F (55 to 58°C). Set aside to rest.

6. Carve venison loin into medallions and serve with Turnip Purée.

Spring

ASPARAGUS

If spring had a mascot, I'm sure it would be asparagus. The happy sight of its tender, cheerful shoots sprouting from a just-thawed ground means that spring has officially arrived. I love asparagus's energetic freshness, as well as its mildly sweet earthiness. And it's surprisingly versatile. You can grill it—check out my Grilled Asparagus Three Ways—or shave it over a beautiful salad, as in my Raw Asparagus Salad with Pine Nuts, Parmesan and Lemon Herb Yogurt. You can try it fried in Asparagus Sesame Fries with Soy Ginger Aïoli, and it's equally wonderful poached in my Shrimp and Grits with Butter Poached White Asparagus. If you want to preserve this springtime gem to enjoy later in the year, I've also got a Pickled Asparagus recipe for you. The options are limitless!

Asparagus purists, rejoice! I've got the hands-down simplest, tastiest and most finger-food-friendly way to nibble on those tender little spears. Simply grill and serve with any one of these three flavourful toppings.

GRILLED ASPARAGUS THREE WAYS

Grill the Asparagus

1. Prepare the grill for direct cooking over medium heat.

2. Toss asparagus with oil, season lightly with salt and pepper and grill until fork-tender and nicely charred. Serve asparagus with topping of your choice.

Gribiche

❶ Makes about ½ cup (125 mL)

¼ cup (60 mL) mayonnaise
1 teaspoon (5 mL) grated lemon zest
1 teaspoon (5 mL) lemon juice
1 teaspoon (5 mL) rinsed and
   chopped capers
1 hard-boiled egg, grated
1 tablespoon (15 mL) finely chopped
   mixed herbs, such as parsley, dill,
   chives, chervil
Kosher salt and cracked black pepper

1. Stir together mayonnaise, lemon zest, lemon juice, capers, egg and herbs until blended. Season to taste with salt and pepper, cover and refrigerate until ready to serve.

❷ Cherry Tomato Basil Salad
Makes about 1½ cups (375 mL)

1½ cups (375 mL) tri-coloured cherry
   tomatoes, halved
1 tablespoon (15 mL) extra-virgin olive
   oil
3 large basil leaves, torn
Pinch of red pepper flakes
Kosher salt and cracked black pepper

1. Toss together tomatoes, oil, basil and red pepper flakes until well mixed. Season to taste with salt and pepper. Let rest at room temperature for 15 minutes to allow flavours to meld.

❸ Bacon Aïoli
Makes about ¾ cup (175 mL)

½ cup (125 mL) mayonnaise
1 tablespoon (15 mL) warm bacon fat
4 slices bacon, fried until crisp and
   finely chopped
1 teaspoon (5 mL) grated lemon zest
1 teaspoon (5 mL) lemon juice
1 teaspoon (5 mL) Dijon mustard
1 clove garlic, minced
Kosher salt and cracked black pepper

1. Whisk together mayonnaise and bacon fat. Whisk in bacon, lemon zest, lemon juice, mustard and garlic until blended. Season to taste with salt and pepper. Cover and refrigerate until ready to serve.

Serves 6

1½ pounds (675 g) asparagus,
   trimmed
2 tablespoons (30 mL) extra-virgin
   olive oil
Kosher salt and cracked black pepper

This is one of my favourite ways to enjoy asparagus when it's at the peak of its season—raw and simply dressed in this fresh and easy salad.

RAW ASPARAGUS SALAD with PINE NUTS, PARMESAN and LEMON HERB YOGURT

Serves 4

Lemon Herb Yogurt

½ cup (125 mL) plain Greek yogurt
2 tablespoons (30 mL) lemon juice
1 teaspoon (5 mL) grated lemon zest
1 teaspoon (5 mL) thyme leaves
2 tablespoons (30 mL) flat-leaf
  parsley leaves
2 tablespoons (30 mL) chopped chives
Kosher salt and cracked black pepper

Raw Asparagus Salad

1 pound (450 g) asparagus, trimmed
4 cups (1 L) frisée leaves
2 tablespoons (30 mL) extra-virgin
  olive oil
Juice of ½ lemon
Kosher salt and cracked black pepper

To Serve

¼ cup (60 mL) shaved Parmesan
  cheese
2 tablespoons (30 mL) toasted pine
  nuts
1 tablespoon (15 mL) finely chopped
  chives

Make the Lemon Herb Yogurt

1. Place yogurt, lemon juice, lemon zest, thyme, parsley and chives in a blender and process until blended. Season to taste with salt and pepper.

Prepare the Raw Asparagus Salad

2. Using a vegetable peeler, slice asparagus spears lengthwise into thin ribbons. Place in a large bowl and add frisée, olive oil and lemon juice. Toss to coat. Season to taste with salt and pepper.

3. Spoon Lemon Herb Yogurt onto a chilled serving dish. Top with asparagus-frisée mixture, then with Parmesan, pine nuts and chives.

I consider this an understated, deeply elegant starter. The mellow sweetness of leeks softly cooked in butter, balanced with tender asparagus— so fresh and bright—finished with luxurious and earthy morel mushrooms. And the lemon crème fraîche? Just a little rich touch to bring it all together. If you can't find morels, feel free to use whatever is available at your grocery store or local market, or leave them out altogether.

ASPARAGUS SOUP with MORELS and LEMON CRÈME FRAÎCHE

Serves 6

Asparagus Soup

2 tablespoons (30 mL) unsalted butter
2 tablespoons (30 mL) olive oil
1 large leek, white and light green
    parts only, halved and thinly sliced
½ cup (125 mL) sliced shallots
2 pounds (900 g) asparagus, trimmed
    and cut into 2-inch (5 cm) lengths
4 cups (1 L) vegetable or chicken stock
Kosher salt and cracked black pepper
2 cups (500 mL) baby spinach

Morels

2 tablespoons (30 mL) unsalted butter
1 cup (250 mL) morel mushrooms,
    washed well, dried and trimmed
2 sprigs thyme
Kosher salt and cracked black pepper
2 tablespoons (30 mL) chopped chives

Lemon Crème Fraîche

¼ cup (60 mL) crème fraîche or sour
    cream
½ teaspoon (2 mL) lemon juice
¼ teaspoon (1 mL) grated lemon zest

To Serve

1 cup (250 mL) cooked spring peas,
    if desired

Make the Asparagus Soup

1. Melt butter with olive oil in a large, heavy saucepan over medium heat. Add leeks and shallots and cook until soft, about 5 minutes. Add asparagus and stock and simmer until asparagus is tender, about 5 minutes. Season soup to taste with salt and pepper. Stir in spinach and remove from heat.

2. Working in batches, purée soup in a blender. Strain back into the pan and keep warm.

Prepare the Morels

3. In a large sauté pan over medium-high heat, combine butter, morels and thyme. Cook for 2 to 3 minutes, then season to taste with salt and pepper. Remove from heat and remove sprigs of thyme. Stir in chives.

Make the Lemon Crème Fraîche

4. In a small bowl, stir together crème fraîche, lemon juice and lemon zest.

5. To serve, divide warm soup among bowls. Top with morels, a dollop of Lemon Crème Fraîche and peas, if using.

Here's a fun and unexpected way to enjoy asparagus, especially when you want to shake things up and yet another salad just won't do. No one can resist a crispy little fry, much less one served with this zippy dipping sauce.

ASPARAGUS SESAME FRIES with SOY GINGER AÏOLI

Make the Soy Ginger Aïoli

1. Whisk together mayonnaise, soy sauce, ginger and cilantro until combined. Cover and refrigerate aïoli until ready to serve.

Make the Asparagus Sesame Fries

2. Place egg whites in a long, narrow dish. In another long, narrow dish, stir together black and white sesame seeds.

3. Working in batches, dip asparagus spears first in egg white, then in sesame seed mixture to coat. Set coated spears aside on a baking sheet.

4. In a large skillet heat 1 inch (2.5 cm) vegetable oil to 350°F (180°C). Working in batches, fry asparagus spears until lightly browned, about 3 minutes, then transfer to paper towel to drain. Season lightly with salt, if using.

5. Serve asparagus fries warm, garnished with green onion and cilantro leaves, and with Soy Ginger Aïoli alongside.

Serves 4

Soy Ginger Aïoli

½ cup (125 mL) mayonnaise
2 teaspoons (10 mL) soy sauce
1 teaspoon (5 mL) grated peeled fresh ginger
1 teaspoon (5 mL) minced cilantro

Asparagus Sesame Fries

2 large egg whites, lightly beaten
¼ cup (60 mL) black sesame seeds
¼ cup (60 mL) white sesame seeds
1 pound (450 g) asparagus, trimmed
Vegetable oil, for frying
Kosher salt, if desired
Thinly sliced green onion, for garnish
Cilantro leaves, for garnish

Shrimp and grits are a classic pair. Here's my take on this iconic dish, using creamy white asparagus to highlight both the texture of the grits and the sweetness of the shrimp. If you have the time, it's worth seeking out Anson Mills grits for this recipe—the quality and flavour of all their products are truly special.

SHRIMP and GRITS with BUTTER POACHED WHITE ASPARAGUS

Serves 4

Grits
2 cups (500 mL) whole milk
2 cups (500 mL) water
1 teaspoon (5 mL) kosher salt
1 cup (250 mL) stone-ground grits
½ cup (125 mL) grated Parmesan cheese
¼ cup (60 mL) unsalted butter
2 tablespoons (30 mL) thinly sliced garlic scapes or green onions
⅛ teaspoon (0.5 mL) cracked black pepper

Butter Poached Asparagus
¼ cup (60 mL) unsalted butter
6 spears thick white asparagus, trimmed

Shrimp
1 pound (450 g) extra-large shrimp (size 16–20), peeled and deveined
Kosher salt and cracked black pepper
¼ cup (60 mL) unsalted butter
2 tablespoons (30 mL) sliced chives

To Serve
Lemon wedges
Chopped chives

Make the Grits
1. In a large saucepan over medium-high heat, bring milk, water and salt to a boil, then gradually whisk in grits until blended. Reduce heat to low, cover and cook until grits are tender, about 45 minutes, stirring frequently.

2. Stir in Parmesan, butter, garlic scapes and black pepper. Keep grits warm until ready to serve.

Poach the Asparagus
3. While grits are cooking, add butter to boiling salted water and cook asparagus for 2 to 3 minutes. Remove from heat. Allow asparagus to rest in poaching liquid for 3 to 4 minutes, then thinly slice on the diagonal.

Prepare the Shrimp
4. Pat shrimp dry with paper towel and season lightly with salt and pepper.

5. In a large skillet over medium-high heat, melt butter. Working in batches if necessary, sauté shrimp until golden brown, about 2 minutes per side. Stir in asparagus and chives. Season well with salt and pepper.

6. To serve, spoon hot grits into a warmed serving bowl and top with shrimp and asparagus mixture. Garnish with lemon wedges and chives and serve immediately.

At harvest time, when there's too much of a good thing, there's a simple solution to avoid waste—pickle it! Here's a great way to preserve all those wonderful bundles of asparagus when they appear en masse at the farmers' market.

PICKLED ASPARAGUS

Makes two 24-ounce (750 mL) jars

2 pounds (900 g) thin to medium-thick asparagus
8 dill sprigs
2 cups (500 mL) white wine vinegar
4 cloves garlic, slivered
¼ cup (60 mL) salt
2 tablespoons (30 mL) granulated sugar
1 tablespoon (15 mL) black pepper-corns
1 tablespoon (15 mL) mustard seeds
1 teaspoon (5 mL) red pepper flakes
¼ teaspoon (1 mL) whole allspice
¼ teaspoon (1 mL) coriander seeds

1. Cut bottoms off asparagus so they fit upright in two 24-ounce (750 mL) containers or jars, with the asparagus tips at least ½ inch (1 cm) below lid. Place asparagus and dill in the jars.

2. In a large saucepan, combine vinegar, garlic, salt, sugar, peppercorns, mustard seeds, red pepper flakes, allspice and coriander seeds. Bring to a boil, then reduce heat and simmer for 10 minutes, stirring to dissolve salt and sugar. Remove from heat and let stand until brine is lukewarm.

3. Pour brine over asparagus. Cover and refrigerate overnight to allow flavours to meld. Keep refrigerated for up to 1 month.

MORELS

Do you find mushrooms as magical as I do? I mean, just look at the magnificent morel, with its lacy, honeycombed cap and distinctly wild nature. Can you imagine the first brave souls to come upon them in a forest and decide to eat them? I'm sure it didn't take long to discover how delicious they are, their nutty, earthy flavour enhanced by a quick fry in a little butter and finished with a touch of cream. Served with a fresh pasta, as in my Pappardelle with Morels and Fava Beans in Cream Sauce, or simply with scrambled eggs, these are one of my favourite mushrooms. I'm so grateful to today's dedicated foragers, whose hard work provides us with baskets of these beauties every spring.

Chefs and mushroom enthusiasts prize the distinctive morel. They are so popular partly because of their very short season, and also because they're incredibly delicious. Here's my version of a springtime Italian bread salad to showcase the beautiful morel.

MOREL MUSHROOM PANZANELLA SALAD

1. Preheat oven to 350°F (180°C) and line a baking sheet with parchment paper.

Sauté the Morels

2. Melt 2 tablespoons (30 mL) butter with olive oil in a large sauté pan over medium heat. Add shallots and toss to coat with butter and oil. Cover and slowly cook shallots, stirring occasionally, for 10 minutes or until softened.

3. Turn heat up to medium-high and begin to caramelize the shallots, stirring constantly, about 10 minutes more. Season with salt and pepper. Remove shallots from the pan and set aside.

4. Return sauté pan to medium-high heat and add remaining 2 tablespoons (30 mL) butter. Add morels and sauté for 3 to 5 minutes, until softened. Add caramelized shallots and blanched fiddleheads. Sauté for another 2 to 3 minutes, until everything is warm. Remove from heat and keep warm.

Make the Sourdough Croutons

5. Melt butter in a small pan over medium heat and cook, stirring often, until golden brown and aromatic, about 3 minutes. Remove from heat.

6. Put the torn bread in a bowl and pour brown butter over them, tossing to coat. Season to taste with salt and pepper and toss again. Spread bread on the baking sheet and bake until croutons are toasted and golden, about 20 minutes, stirring occasionally.

Make the Grainy Mustard Dressing

7. While croutons are baking, whisk together Dijon mustard, whole-grain mustard, honey and vinegar until well combined. Slowly whisk in canola oil, then olive oil, until emulsified. Season to taste with salt and pepper. Keep refrigerated for up to 1 month.

Assemble the Salad

8. Transfer warm morel mixture to a large bowl. Add Sourdough Croutons and watercress. Dress with ½ cup (125 mL) Grainy Mustard Dressing. Mix well and season to taste with salt and pepper. Serve immediately.

Serves 4

Sautéed Morels

4 tablespoons (60 mL) unsalted butter, divided
1 tablespoon (15 mL) olive oil
4 shallots, cut lengthwise into quarters
Kosher salt and cracked black pepper
3 cups (750 mL) morel mushrooms, washed well, dried and trimmed
½ cup (125 mL) fiddleheads, blanched

Sourdough Croutons

3 tablespoons (45 mL) unsalted butter
2 cups (500 mL) torn sourdough bread
Kosher salt and cracked black pepper

Grainy Mustard Dressing
Makes 1¼ cups (300 mL)

2 tablespoons (30 mL) Dijon mustard
2 tablespoons (30 mL) whole-grain mustard (I like Kozlik's Triple Crunch Mustard)
2 tablespoons (30 mL) honey
¼ cup (60 mL) white wine vinegar
½ cup (125 mL) canola oil
¼ cup (60 mL) extra-virgin olive oil
Kosher salt and cracked black pepper

To Serve

2 cups (500 mL) watercress, washed and trimmed
Kosher salt and cracked black pepper

If you're a fan of morel mushrooms, you'll want to try this creamy pasta dish. Foraged morels, pancetta, cream, Parmesan and perfect fava beans—a combination that is as decadent as it is delicious. This could quite possibly be one of the best recipes in this book!

PAPPARDELLE with MORELS and FAVA BEANS in CREAM SAUCE

Serves 6

1½ cups (375 mL) shelled fava beans (about 2 pounds/900 g pods)
1 tablespoon (15 mL) unsalted butter
1 tablespoon (15 mL) olive oil
¼ cup (60 mL) finely diced pancetta (about 2 ounces/55 g)
2 shallots, finely diced
2 cups (500 mL) well-cleaned and thinly sliced morel mushrooms
1½ cups (375 mL) heavy (35%) cream
Kosher salt and cracked black pepper
1 pound (450 g) pappardelle
1 cup (250 mL) grated Parmesan cheese
2 tablespoons (30 mL) finely chopped chives

1. In a large pot of boiling salted water, cook fava beans for 1 minute. Using a large slotted spoon, remove beans to a colander set over a large bowl. Reserve the blanching water to cook the pasta.

2. Rinse fava beans under cold running water until cool. Using your fingers or a paring knife, carefully tear open the outer hull of each bean. Gently squeeze the fava beans into a small bowl.

3. In a large sauté pan, melt butter with olive oil over medium heat. Add pancetta and cook, stirring occasionally, for 2 to 3 minutes. Add shallots and morels, increase heat to medium-high, and cook, stirring occasion-ally, until the liquid released from the mushrooms has been reabsorbed, 3 to 4 minutes.

4. Reduce heat to medium and add fava beans, cream, and salt and pepper to taste. Cook, stirring occasionally, until sauce has thickened slightly, 3 to 4 minutes. Turn off the heat and adjust seasoning as needed.

5. Return the blanching water to a boil. Add pappardelle and cook accord-ing to package directions until al dente. Drain pasta and add to sauce. Turn the heat to medium-high, add Parmesan and chives, and gently toss noodles with the sauce until heated through. Serve immediately.

NEW POTATOES

When I was growing up, I especially looked forward to Sunday suppers in the spring. Whether we were having a roast leg of lamb or a maple-glazed ham, there would always be boiled new potatoes slathered in butter and herbs. To me there is nothing better than Salt-Baked New Potatoes with Arugula Butter. I could eat them every day. New potatoes have a wonderful sweetness and a fluffy texture that I think are perfect with absolutely everything, especially bacon, eggs, cheese and herbs. They're a great choice for hashes, like my Kielbasa Potato Hash with Sunny-Side-Up Eggs, and salads, especially the Warm Potato Salad with Bacon and Triple Crunch Mustard Vinaigrette, when you want to add a little extra colour and texture in the mix.

The reason new potatoes are so tasty is their delicate, paper-thin skin, which makes the potato taste sweeter, unlike the earthiness of a thicker-skinned potato. To complement the sweetness, I like to serve these with arugula butter, which has wonderful peppery notes. Salt baking is a fantastic way to prepare these potatoes because it helps keep their flesh nice and fluffy.

SALT-BAKED NEW POTATOES with ARUGULA BUTTER

1. Preheat oven to 350°F (180°C).

2. Sprinkle salt in an even layer on a rimmed baking sheet and set potatoes on top. Bake until fork-tender, about 45 minutes.

3. Meanwhile, using a mortar and pestle or a small food processor, mash or process arugula with butter until smooth.

4. Brush off any excess salt sticking to the potatoes. Toss potatoes in arugula butter while still warm. Season to taste with salt and pepper.

Serves 4

1 cup (250 mL) kosher salt
1½ pounds (675 g) small new
    potatoes, scrubbed and patted dry
½ cup (125 mL) coarsely chopped
    packed arugula
¼ cup (60 mL) unsalted butter, at
    room temperature
Kosher salt and cracked black pepper

A hash is a classic and comforting dish consisting of diced or chopped meat, potatoes and spices all mixed together and fried. On Sunday mornings at home, I like to make this breakfast hash using kielbasa sausage and topped with a runny sunny-side-up egg. It's a delicious way to start the day!

KIELBASA POTATO HASH with SUNNY-SIDE-UP EGGS

Serves 4

1 pound (450 g) mini new potatoes
2 teaspoons (10 mL) canola oil
¼ pound (115 g) kielbasa, cut into
    ¼-inch (5 mm) rounds
2 tablespoons (30 mL) unsalted
    butter, divided
4 spring onions, halved lengthwise
4 large eggs
Kosher salt and cracked black pepper

1. In a saucepan, cover potatoes with cold water and bring to a boil over high heat. Reduce heat to medium and cook until potatoes are fork-tender, about 15 minutes. Drain potatoes, let cool for 5 minutes, then cut in half.

2. Meanwhile, preheat oven to 325°F (160°C). In a medium skillet over medium heat, add oil and kielbasa and cook until sausage is golden brown, about 15 minutes, stirring occasionally. Transfer kielbasa to a large ovenproof plate and keep warm in the oven.

3. Melt 1 tablespoon (15 mL) butter in the skillet over medium heat. Arrange reserved potatoes in a single layer cut side down, in batches if necessary, and cook until golden brown, about 10 minutes. Transfer to plate with kielbasa and keep warm.

4. In the skillet, arrange spring onions cut side down and cook until golden, about 2 minutes. Transfer to plate with kielbasa-potato mixture and keep warm.

5. Melt remaining 1 tablespoon (15 mL) butter in skillet. Break in eggs, season with salt and pepper, and cook just until white has set, about 3 minutes for sunny-side-up.

6. To serve, divide kielbasa-potato mixture and spring onions among warmed plates. Top with fried eggs and serve immediately.

This is potato salad 2.0, and it's a wonderful one to serve once the weather turns warm in the spring. The cooked potatoes are tossed with a vinaigrette, soaking up all the goodness and flavours of the mustard, vinegar and bacon.

WARM POTATO SALAD with BACON and TRIPLE CRUNCH MUSTARD VINAIGRETTE

1. In a saucepan, cover potatoes with cold water and bring to a boil over high heat. Reduce heat to medium and cook until fork-tender, about 15 minutes. Drain well and transfer to a bowl.

2. Meanwhile, in a medium skillet over medium heat, fry bacon until crisp, about 15 minutes. Transfer to paper towel to drain.

3. Whisk together oil, vinegar and mustard until blended. Season to taste with salt and pepper.

4. Break crispy bacon crosswise into ½-inch (1 cm) pieces and add to potatoes. Add vinaigrette and toss until well coated. Spoon potato salad onto a serving plate and garnish with chopped herbs.

Serves 6

2 pounds (900 g) tri-coloured mini potatoes
6 slices bacon
¼ cup (60 mL) canola oil
2 tablespoons (30 mL) apple cider vinegar
1 tablespoon (15 mL) whole-grain mustard (I like Kozlik's Triple Crunch Mustard)
Kosher salt and cracked black pepper
¼ cup (60 mL) mixed chopped herbs, such as dill, chervil and chives, for garnish

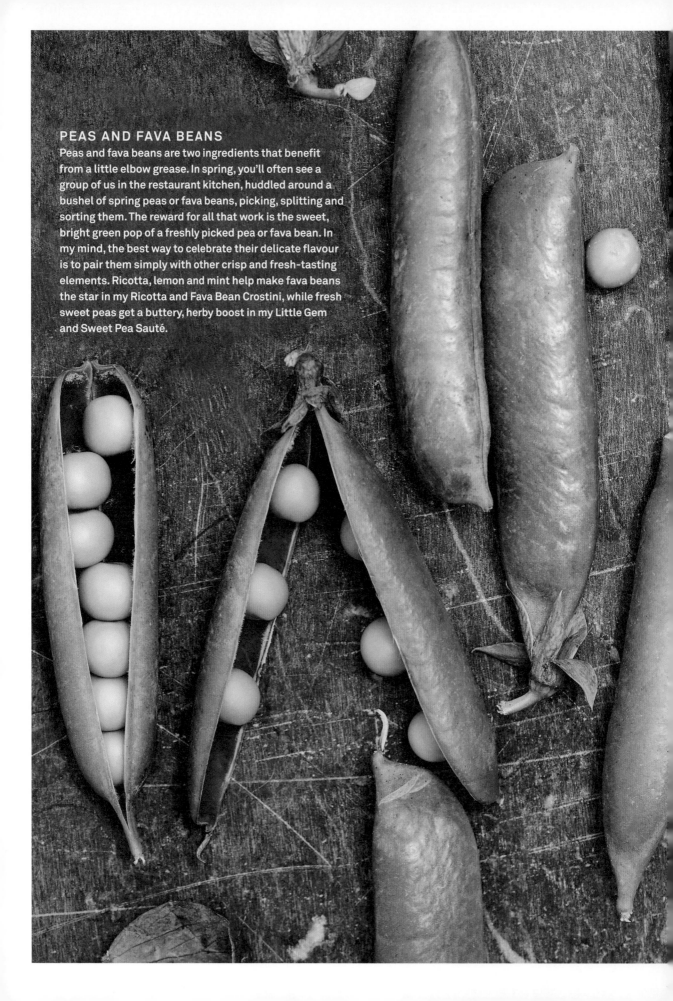

PEAS AND FAVA BEANS

Peas and fava beans are two ingredients that benefit from a little elbow grease. In spring, you'll often see a group of us in the restaurant kitchen, huddled around a bushel of spring peas or fava beans, picking, splitting and sorting them. The reward for all that work is the sweet, bright green pop of a freshly picked pea or fava bean. In my mind, the best way to celebrate their delicate flavour is to pair them simply with other crisp and fresh-tasting elements. Ricotta, lemon and mint help make fava beans the star in my Ricotta and Fava Bean Crostini, while fresh sweet peas get a buttery, herby boost in my Little Gem and Sweet Pea Sauté.

We don't often think about cooking lettuce, which is a shame, since the gentle heat works wonders to enhance the naturally delicate flavours of these beautiful spring ingredients. I highly recommend you give it a try! This is a perfect side dish to the Sockeye Salmon Poached in a Spring Vegetable Nage (page 200).

LITTLE GEM and SWEET PEA SAUTÉ

Serves 4

8 slices bacon
4 Little Gem lettuces, halved
    lengthwise
½ cup (125 mL) chicken stock or
    water
1 cup (250 mL) sweet peas
¼ cup (60 mL) unsalted butter
2 teaspoons (10 mL) finely chopped
    tarragon
Kosher salt and cracked black pepper

1. In a skillet over medium heat, fry bacon until crispy, then transfer to paper towel to drain. Remove all but 2 tablespoons (30 mL) bacon fat from skillet. Add lettuces cut side down and cook until golden, about 5 minutes, turning only once. Place lettuces cut side up on a serving platter.

2. Add stock, peas and butter to the skillet. Cook until peas are tender, 3 to 4 minutes, stirring occasionally. Stir in tarragon and season to taste with salt and pepper.

3. Spoon buttered peas over the lettuce and garnish with bacon slices.

Yes, fava beans do need a little attention—with a first cook in salted water, followed by a second going over to remove their tough outer jackets—but a little patience, and ideally a pair of helping hands, pays off, and the results are so worth it. One or two crostini would make an easy, fresh lunch alongside a bowl of soup, while a platter full would be a wonderful casual dinner starter for a larger group, glasses of crisp white wine in hand.

RICOTTA and FAVA BEAN CROSTINI

Makes 8 crostini

Toast the Crostini

1. Set oven to broil or preheat a grill to medium-high heat.

2. Rub slices of baguette with garlic cloves and brush lightly with olive oil on both sides. Lightly toast under a hot broiler or on a hot grill. Set aside.

Make the Fava Topping

3. In a large pot of boiling salted water, cook fava beans until tender, 2 to 3 minutes. Drain and let cool, then carefully peel off the tough outer skin from each bean.

4. Heat 1 tablespoon (15 mL) olive oil in a medium sauté pan over medium-high heat. Add green onions and sauté for 1 minute, until wilted. Stir in fava beans and cook for 2 minutes or until warmed through.

5. Transfer the fava mixture to a medium bowl. Add remaining 2 tablespoons (30 mL) olive oil, lemon juice, lemon zest and mint, then toss until combined. Mash slightly with the back of a fork. Season to taste with salt and pepper.

Make the Ricotta Topping

6. Stir ricotta and Parmesan together in a small bowl. Season to taste with salt and pepper.

7. Arrange toasts on a serving platter. Spread each slice with ricotta, then spoon fava mixture on top. Drizzle with a bit more olive oil and serve immediately.

Crostini

8 slices crusty baguette (cut ¾ inch/2 cm on the diagonal)
2 cloves garlic, cut in half
2 tablespoons (30 mL) olive oil

Fava Topping

1½ cups (375 mL) shelled fava beans (from about 2 pounds/900 g pods)
3 tablespoons (45 mL) olive oil, divided
¼ cup (60 mL) finely chopped green onions
2 tablespoons (30 mL) lemon juice
½ teaspoon (2 mL) grated lemon zest
2 tablespoons (30 mL) coarsely chopped mint
Kosher salt and cracked black pepper

Ricotta Topping

1 cup (250 mL) ricotta cheese
¼ cup (60 mL) grated Parmesan cheese
Kosher salt and cracked black pepper

To my mind, this is the ideal springtime weekend lunch. You've come home from the market to prepare a little edible celebration, inviting a few friends over to join in. This recipe is elegant enough for company and easily serves a small group, yet it's simple to prepare and satisfyingly light enough that you can go about the rest of your day with ease. Serve with Little Gem and Sweet Pea Sauté (page 196), set out a crunchy baguette with some sweet butter on the table, and you're all set. If you've never tried sea beans (also known as sea asparagus), I highly recommend you do so here. This unique vegetable is salty like the sea and a wonderful addition to the dish.

SOCKEYE SALMON POACHED in a SPRING VEGETABLE NAGE

Serves 4

1 side sockeye salmon (about
   3 pounds/1.35 kg), skin and pin
   bones removed
6 cups (1.5 L) water
2 cups (500 mL) dry white wine
4 spring onions, sliced in half
1 lemon, thinly sliced
4 bay leaves
4 sprigs thyme
4 sprigs dill
1 tablespoon (15 mL) tarragon leaves
½ cup (125 mL) chopped asparagus
½ cup (125 mL) chopped green beans
¼ cup (60 mL) chopped sea beans
¼ cup (60 mL) sweet peas
1 teaspoon (5 mL) kosher salt

1. Place salmon in a large, deep skillet and add water, white wine, onions, lemon, bay leaves, thyme, dill, tarragon, asparagus, green beans, sea beans, sweet peas and salt. Salmon should be submerged in poaching liquid. Add more water if necessary.

2. Set skillet over medium-low heat and bring to a gentle simmer. Poach, uncovered, until internal temperature reaches 130°F (55°C) and flesh flakes easily with a fork, about 20 minutes.

3. Serve salmon in bowls, with vegetable nage and poached vegetables spooned over top.

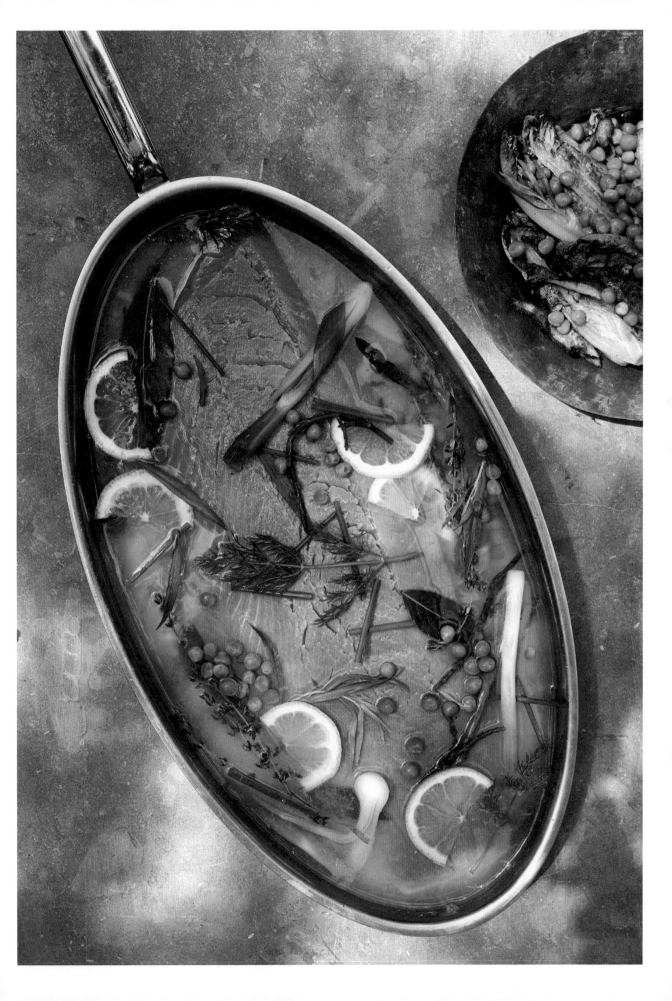

RADISHES

Radishes freshly picked from the garden hold a special spot in my heart. They are just about the quickest and easiest vegetables to grow in the spring, and I always feel unreasonably accomplished when they arrive! I'll keep a bright pink and white handful standing in icy cold water on the kitchen counter, tender leaves and all. The thing is to have a stick of sweet butter nearby, with a small bowl of crunchy Maldon sea salt; some bread, of course, would be good here too. The refreshing zing of a crunchy, cold peppery radish, a smear of good butter, and a pinch of salt is the perfect snack. Not only wonderful raw, they're delicious served warm in my Honey-Roasted Radishes with Dill and Wild Onion Flowers.

Radishes are generally eaten raw, but when rethinking how to prepare this spring staple, I decided to break from tradition and roast them in honey. What happens to radishes when they're cooked? Their characteristic peppery bite mellows, and they get sweeter and juicier. These are perfectly delicious on their own, or try mixing them with other roasted vegetables such as carrots, fennel or potatoes.

HONEY-ROASTED RADISHES with DILL and WILD ONION FLOWERS

1. Position a rack in the centre of the oven and set a 12-inch (30 cm) cast-iron pan on the rack. Preheat the oven to 450°F (230°C).

2. In a medium bowl, combine the honey, butter, cider vinegar, salt and pepper. Add the radishes and toss until coated. Transfer to the hot pan and spread in a single layer. Roast, stirring occasionally, until the radishes are crisp-tender, 15 to 20 minutes.

3. Remove from the oven. Top with chopped dill and garnish with the onion flowers, if using.

Serves 4

3 tablespoons (45 mL) honey
1 tablespoon (15 mL) unsalted butter, melted
1 tablespoon (15 mL) apple cider vinegar
½ teaspoon (2 mL) kosher salt
½ teaspoon (2 mL) cracked black pepper
2 cups (500 mL) red garden radishes, trimmed and quartered lengthwise
2 tablespoons (30 mL) chopped dill
8 onion flowers, for garnish, if desired

This is a classic French way of serving radishes, simple and yet so good. The watery, crisp bite of the radishes contrasted with the creamy richness of the ramp butter and the crackly dry crunch of the salt is a match made in heaven.

RADISH SANDWICHES with RAMP BUTTER

Serves 6 to 8

Ramp Butter
Makes about 2 cups (500 mL)

½ pound (225 g) ramps, bulbs removed (about 20 ramps)
1 pound (450 g) unsalted butter, at room temperature
2 teaspoons (10 mL) honey
Grated zest and juice of 1 lemon
Kosher salt and cracked black pepper

Radish Sandwiches
1 baguette, cut in half horizontally
2 cloves garlic, cut in half
2 tablespoons (30 mL) olive oil
12 radishes, very thinly sliced
Kosher salt and cracked black pepper
Basil seedlings or leaves, for garnish
Maldon sea salt and cracked black pepper

Make the Ramp Butter

1. Blanch ramps in boiling salted water for 1 minute. Transfer to a bowl of ice water. Drain and squeeze out excess water. Spread ramps on paper towel and pat dry.

2. Coarsely chop ramps and place in a food processor along with the butter, honey and lemon zest and juice. Process until butter is smooth. Season to taste with salt and pepper. Store in an airtight container in the refrigerator for up to 1 week or freeze for up to 2 months.

Assemble the Radish Sandwiches

3. Set oven to broil or preheat a grill to medium-high heat.

4. Rub cut sides of baguette with garlic cloves and brush lightly with olive oil. Lightly toast under a hot broiler or on a hot grill.

5. Toss radishes with salt and pepper to taste in a medium bowl. Spread Ramp Butter on each half of baguette. Top bottom half of baguette with radish slices and basil; season with sea salt and pepper. Top with other half of baguette, cut on the diagonal into small sandwiches and serve.

RHUBARB

We had two huge rhubarb plants in our backyard when I was growing up. Every spring we'd watch as their fans grew up and out, and we'd dip the early pink stalks in sugar and crunch on them like the best sour candy. Nowadays, for the restaurant, we make a gorgeous rhubarb shrub for one of our signature drinks, Ruby's Ginny Rhubarb Fizz. We also channel that sweet-tart flavour into killer jams, including my Gingered Rhubarb Jam, or a vinaigrette, which I show you how to make in my Chicken Leg Confit with Frisée and Spring Onion Salad with Rhubarb Vinaigrette. If you catch me in the kitchen, though, don't be surprised if you see me snacking on some extra rhubarb bits with a bowl of sugar nearby.

This gingered rhubarb jam is so versatile. I love serving it with cheese, but it's also great on top of a big bowl of ice cream or a nice piece of grilled fish. The ginger helps balance the natural tartness of the rhubarb in this well-rounded and delicious preserve.

GINGERED RHUBARB JAM

1. In a large, heavy skillet, combine rhubarb, sugar, ginger, lemon juice, lemon zest and vanilla. Bring to a simmer over medium-high heat and cook, stirring often, for about 8 minutes or until the juices thicken slightly and the rhubarb is falling apart.

2. Serve warm, or let cool and refrigerate in an airtight container for up to 1 week.

Makes 3 cups (750 mL)

4 cups (1 L) rhubarb cut into ½-inch (1 cm) pieces
1 cup (250 mL) granulated sugar
¼ cup (60 mL) grated peeled fresh ginger
2 tablespoons (30 mL) lemon juice
1 teaspoon (5 mL) grated lemon zest
1½ teaspoons (7 mL) pure vanilla extract

When it's rhubarb season, our talented chefs at Ruby Watchco switch into high gear. Pies, tarts, cakes, relishes, chutneys, compotes, sauces, vinaigrettes, sorbets and, yes, shrubs! A shrub is a fruit syrup, a way of preserving fruits that are in season with vinegar and other flavourings. Making shrubs at home is an excellent way of enjoying the bountiful harvest of any fruit. In addition to drinks, you can use shrubs in salad dressings and jams or as a glaze on meats. One of the most popular cocktails on our menu is this rhubarb fizz. Now you can make it at home! Be sure to make lots of this lovely pink rhubarb syrup, so you can sip this drink throughout the spring.

RUBY'S GINNY RHUBARB FIZZ

Make the Rhubarb Shrub

1. Combine rhubarb, lemon zest, ginger, sugar and vinegar in a heavy saucepan. Bring to a boil, then reduce heat and simmer very gently for 30 to 40 minutes, stirring occasionally, until the fruit is soft.

2. Set a fine-mesh sieve over a large bowl. Pour rhubarb through the sieve and leave to drain, without pressing on the fruit. Carefully pour syrup into a clean bottle, cover and refrigerate for up to 1 month.

Prepare the Cocktail

3. In a rocks glass, stir together Rhubarb Shrub and gin. Add ice, top with soda water and squeeze in a lemon wedge. Stir again and enjoy!

Serves 1

Rhubarb Shrub
Makes about 1 cup (250 mL), enough
  for 8 cocktails
4 cups (1 L) rhubarb chopped into
  ½-inch (1 cm) pieces
2 strips lemon zest
2-inch (5 cm) piece fresh ginger,
  peeled and thinly sliced
2½ cups (625 mL) granulated sugar
2 cups (500 mL) white vinegar

Ruby's Ginny Rhubarb Fizz
1 ounce (30 mL) Rhubarb Shrub
2 ounces (60 mL) gin
Soda water
Lemon wedge

This fun play on classic duck confit instead uses chicken and skips the salt curing. The chicken is poached low and slow in olive oil flavoured with spring onions, rhubarb, lemon and thyme—a wonderfully fresh spring combination. The result is an incredibly tender and flavourful dish.

CHICKEN LEG CONFIT with FRISÉE and SPRING ONION SALAD with RHUBARB VINAIGRETTE

Serves 4

Rhubarb Vinaigrette
Makes about 2 cups (500 mL)
1 cup (250 mL) olive oil
½ cup (125 mL) diced rhubarb
2 cloves garlic, minced
Grated zest of 1 orange
½ cup (125 mL) freshly squeezed
    orange juice
½ cup (125 mL) rice vinegar
2 tablespoons (30 mL) honey
Kosher salt and cracked black pepper

Chicken Leg Confit
½ cup (125 mL) extra-virgin olive oil
3 tablespoons (45 mL) honey
2 to 4 spring onions, cut in half
    crosswise and tops cut into 2-inch
    (5 cm) pieces
2 stalks rhubarb, cut into 1-inch
    (2.5 cm) pieces
Grated zest and juice of 1 lemon
4 sprigs thyme
1 serrano chili, seeded and coarsely
    chopped
2 bay leaves
Kosher salt and cracked black pepper
4 chicken legs

Frisée and Spring Onion Salad
Leaves from 2 heads frisée, cleaned
    and dried
½ cup (125 mL) Pickled Spring Onions
    (page 221), halved or quartered
½ cup (125 mL) toasted almonds,
    chopped
1 bunch green onions, finely chopped
Kosher salt and cracked black pepper

Make the Rhubarb Vinaigrette
1. In a skillet, heat 2 teaspoons (10 mL) oil over medium-high heat. Add rhubarb and sauté for 3 to 4 minutes. Stir in garlic, orange zest and juice and simmer for a few minutes. Pour rhubarb mixture into a blender and add rice vinegar and honey. With the blender running, add remaining oil in a steady stream. Season to taste with salt and pepper. Vinaigrette can be stored in a mason jar in the refrigerator for up to 2 weeks.

Prepare the Chicken Leg Confit
2. In a medium bowl, combine olive oil, honey, onions, rhubarb, lemon zest and juice, thyme, chili, bay leaves, salt and pepper; stir together well. Add chicken thighs and mix around until all the chicken is coated. Cover with plastic wrap and marinate in the refrigerator for at least 1 hour or overnight.

3. Preheat oven to 375°F (190°C).

4. Pour chicken and the marinade into a small baking dish and arrange so chicken is in a single layer. Bake for 25 to 35 minutes, until chicken is cooked through. Let chicken rest, covered with foil, for 10 minutes or so.

Make the Frisée and Spring Onion Salad
5. While chicken is resting, toss frisée, pickled onions, almonds and green onions in a large bowl. Dress salad with ½ cup (125 mL) Rhubarb Vinaigrette and season to taste with salt and pepper.

6. Serve Chicken Leg Confit with pan juices and Frisée and Spring Onion Salad.

SPRING GREENS AND HERBS

Most spring greens are a bit shy. What I mean by that is, for example, tender pea shoots or delicate, buttery lettuces are sweet, young versions of the "grown-up" greens they will become later in the season. What I love about these ingredients—spring dandelion and garlic scapes come to mind—is that in their early stages, they contain all their vibrant, direct flavour without all the bitterness that often comes with maturity. I particularly love the earthy freshness of these greens in my Pasta with Dandelion Greens, Chorizo and Manchego. You'll see these young greens and herbs, like chervil, dill and parsley, appear in local markets only as the spring season gets under way, so it's well worth seeking them out for a special treat.

Dandelion greens are a member of the sunflower family and are considered a bitter green. They can be used anytime you are making something that calls for a hearty green like kale or chard. The richness of this salad comes from the garlic confit dressing. The salad is then topped with crispy white anchovies, making it an incredible Caesar. To save you a little time, make the dressing up to a week ahead.

DANDELION CAESAR SALAD with CRISPY ANCHOVY CROUTONS and GARLIC CONFIT DRESSING

Serves 4

Garlic Confit

2 heads garlic, cloves separated and peeled (at least 14 cloves)
2 sprigs thyme
2 bay leaves
1 cup (250 mL) olive oil

Garlic Confit Dressing
Makes 1 cup (250 mL)

10 confit garlic cloves
¾ cup (175 mL) garlic-infused or regular olive oil
¼ cup (60 mL) sherry vinegar
2 tablespoons (30 mL) lemon juice
1 teaspoon (5 mL) dark brown sugar
Kosher salt and cracked black pepper

Aïoli
Makes about ½ cup (125 mL)

3 to 4 confit garlic cloves
Kosher salt
2 large egg yolks
2 tablespoons (30 mL) lemon juice
1 teaspoon (5 mL) Dijon mustard
¼ cup (60 mL) extra-virgin olive oil
3 tablespoons (45 mL) canola oil
Cracked black pepper

Crispy Anchovy Croutons

4 cups (1 L) canola oil, for frying
1 cup (250 mL) all-purpose flour
Kosher salt and cracked black pepper
12 white anchovy fillets, drained

Salad

4 cups (1 L) dandelion greens, washed and trimmed
Kosher salt and cracked black pepper
Parmesan cheese

Prepare the Garlic Confit

1. In a small saucepan, combine garlic cloves, thyme, bay leaves and olive oil. Make sure the olive oil completely covers the garlic. Cook over as low a heat as possible for 30 to 40 minutes, until garlic cloves are golden brown and very tender. Allow garlic and oil to cool to room temperature.

Make the Garlic Confit Dressing

2. In a blender or food processor, combine confit garlic cloves, oil, vinegar, lemon juice and sugar. Blend or pulse until dressing is emulsified. Season well with salt and pepper. Refrigerate in an airtight container for up to 1 week.

Make the Aïoli

3. Mince confit garlic cloves, then mash to a paste with a pinch of salt using the side of a large, heavy knife.

4. In a bowl, whisk together egg yolks, lemon juice and mustard in a bowl. Combine olive and canola oils and add, a few drops at a time, to yolk mixture, whisking constantly, until all oil is incorporated and mixture is emulsified. Whisk in garlic paste and season to taste with salt and pepper. Chill, covered, until ready to use.

Prepare the Crispy Anchovy Croutons

5. In a large, deep saucepan, heat 2 inches (5 cm) oil to 350°F (180°C).

6. In a bowl, mix together flour, salt and pepper. Dredge half of anchovies in flour mixture, tossing to coat well. Transfer to a sieve and shake to remove excess flour. Fry, stirring frequently to separate, until golden, about 3 minutes, then transfer with a slotted spoon to paper towel to drain. Repeat with remaining anchovies.

Assemble the Salad

7. In a large bowl, toss the dandelion greens with ½ cup (125 mL) Garlic Confit Dressing. Season with salt and pepper.

8. Place a large spoonful of aïoli on each salad plate and use the back of the spoon to spread aïoli into a large circle. Divide dressed greens among plates, placing them in the middle of the aïoli. Shave Parmesan over each salad and garnish with Crispy Anchovy Croutons.

This is one of my favourite go-to pastas—it's so quick and easy to make. Dandelion greens pair so wonderfully with chorizo, chilies, garlic and lots of cheese. I love using chorizo sausage here, but if you can't get your hands on any, Italian sausage or bacon would be amazing too.

PASTA with DANDELION GREENS, CHORIZO and MANCHEGO

1. In a large saucepan over medium heat, heat 2 tablespoons (30 mL) oil. Add chorizo and cook for 3 to 5 minutes, or until the meat is cooked, stirring often. Add the remaining 2 tablespoons (30 mL) oil and lower the heat to medium-low. When the oil is warm, add chilies and garlic and cook for 2 minutes, stirring occasionally. Turn off the heat and let stand for 5 minutes.

2. Meanwhile, in a large pot of boiling salted water, cook pasta according to package directions until al dente.

3. Drain pasta and add to warm chorizo mixture. Add dandelion greens, parsley and lemon zest and juice. Mix well. Season to taste with salt and pepper. Serve pasta immediately, topped with grated Manchego.

Serves 4 to 6

4 tablespoons (60 mL) olive oil, divided

2 fresh chorizo sausages, meat removed from casings

2 small red chilies, seeded and finely chopped

3 cloves garlic, finely minced

1 pound (450 g) pasta, whichever shape you desire

2 cups (500 mL) dandelion greens, washed and coarsely chopped

2 tablespoons (30 mL) chopped flat-leaf parsley

Grated zest and juice of ½ lemon

Kosher salt and cracked black pepper

¾ cup (175 mL) grated Manchego cheese

This really is a delicious, quick meal: the chicken will be tender and sautés quickly. Then there's the lemon, tarragon and butter all swirled together into a wonderful dressing, with your favourite spring vegetables. A perfect spring dinner! If you can't find morels, chanterelle or oyster mushrooms would be perfect alternatives.

CHICKEN BREASTS with MORELS, ASPARAGUS and LEMON HERB DRESSING

Serves 4

1 bunch asparagus, trimmed and cut
   on the diagonal into 2-inch (5 cm)
   lengths
½ cup (125 mL) sweet peas
½ cup (125 mL) shelled fava beans
4 skinless, boneless chicken breasts,
   butterflied
Kosher salt and cracked black pepper
2 tablespoons (30 mL) olive oil,
   divided
2 tablespoons (30 mL) unsalted butter
2 shallots, finely diced
1 cup (250 mL) morel mushrooms,
   washed well, dried and cut in half
2 to 4 radishes, thinly sliced
2 tablespoons (30 mL) coarsely
   chopped tarragon
2 tablespoons (30 mL) lemon juice
Lemon wedges, for garnish, if desired

1. In a saucepan of boiling salted water, blanch asparagus for 1 minute. With a slotted spoon, transfer to a bowl of ice water to stop the cooking process. Drain asparagus, pat dry with paper towel and transfer to a small bowl. Blanch and cool the peas the same way, and add to asparagus. Lastly, blanch and cool the fava beans the same way. Using your fingers or a paring knife, carefully tear open the outer hull of each bean. Gently squeeze out the fava beans and add to asparagus and peas.

2. Season chicken on both sides with salt and pepper. Heat 1 tablespoon (15 mL) olive oil in a large skillet over medium-high heat. Add 2 chicken breasts and sauté until golden brown and cooked through, 2 to 3 minutes per side. Transfer to serving plates and cover with foil. Add remaining 1 tablespoon (15 mL) olive oil to pan if needed and repeat with remaining chicken breasts.

3. In the same skillet over medium heat, add butter, shallots and morels. Sauté until morels are tender, 3 to 4 minutes. Stir in blanched asparagus, peas and fava beans and cook, stirring, until heated through, about 3 minutes. Season with salt and pepper.

4. Remove from heat and toss in radishes, tarragon and lemon juice. Spoon over chicken, and garnish with lemon wedges, if using.

SPRING ONIONS AND RAMPS

Every spring, a few weeks after the last snow has cleared and the sun has encouraged all sorts of new growth, we'll pack up the dogs and head out to pick ramps. We love gathering these intensely garlicky wild leeks, as they're a sure sign that spring has arrived. After cleaning and trimming them, the real fun begins—cooking them in as many ways as we can. I might preserve them into Pickled Ramps or whip up a pesto for my Primavera Pizza with Ramp Pesto. Of course, if you don't have wild ramps available in your neck of the woods, spring onions make a great substitute. They have a softer onion flavour but are just as versatile. When eaten raw, both have an unmistakable, pleasantly pungent kick; grilling and frying help to tame that bite into a mellow, crowd-friendly flavour.

This quick little pickle is a great way to preserve that extra bunch of fresh spring onions lurking in your crisper. They add a bright zip to salads and dressings, keep well for weeks and only take minutes to make.

PICKLED SPRING ONIONS

1. Divide onions between two 1-pint (500 mL) mason jars.

2. In a saucepan, combine vinegar, water, sugar and salt. Bring to a boil over high heat, stirring until sugar and salt dissolve. Add garlic, thyme and peppercorns, reduce heat to low and simmer for 2 or 3 minutes.

3. Pour the pickling liquid over the onions and cover the jars with lids. Let cool to room temperature then refrigerate overnight. These will keep in the refrigerator for 3 weeks.

Makes two 1-pint (500 mL) jars

2 cups (500 mL) spring onions or pearl
    onions, peeled
¾ cup (175 mL) rice vinegar
½ cup (125 mL) water
¼ cup (60 mL) granulated sugar
1 tablespoon (15 mL) kosher salt
1 clove garlic, halved
1 teaspoon (5 mL) fresh thyme leaves
½ teaspoon (2 mL) black peppercorns

I love to fire up the wood-burning oven at home for an impromptu pizza party with friends. In the spring everyone asks for this classic springtime combination of morels, fiddleheads, ramp pesto and a beautiful creamy buffalo mozzarella. This pizza is a wonderful celebration of spring produce and a real crowd-pleaser. If morels aren't available, any type of mushroom will work.

PRIMAVERA PIZZA with RAMP PESTO

Makes 6 individual pizzas

Basil Ramp Pesto
Makes about 3 cups (750 mL)
½ cup (125 mL) toasted walnuts
3 cups (750 mL) packed fresh basil
    leaves
4 to 6 ramps, cleaned well (or 1 bunch
    of green onions)
¾ to 1 cup (175 to 250 mL) extra-
    virgin olive oil
1 cup (250 mL) grated pecorino or
    Parmesan cheese
Kosher salt and cracked black pepper

Pizza Dough
1 cup (250 mL) lukewarm water
1 tablespoon (15 mL) honey
4 teaspoons (22 mL) active dry yeast
2½ cups (625 mL) all-purpose flour
¼ cup (60 mL) olive oil
1 teaspoon (5 mL) salt

Morel and Fiddlehead Topping
1 tablespoon (15 mL) olive oil
2 tablespoons (30 mL) unsalted butter
2 small shallots, thinly sliced
½ pound (225 g) morel mushrooms,
    washed well, dried and cut in half
    lengthwise
½ pound (225 g) fiddleheads, washed
    and dried
1 teaspoon (5 mL) chopped thyme
Kosher salt and cracked black pepper

For Assembly
Cornmeal, for dusting
Olive oil, for brushing
1 ball (8 ounces/225 g) buffalo
    mozzarella

Make the Basil Ramp Pesto
1. In a food processor, chop walnuts for 30 seconds or until finely chopped. Add basil leaves and ramps. With processor running, slowly pour oil through the feed tube and process until pesto is thoroughly puréed. Add the pecorino and process for a just a second to mix. Season to taste with salt and pepper. Store pesto in the refrigerator with a thin film of olive oil on top until ready to use.

Make the Pizza Dough
2. In a medium bowl, stir together water, honey and yeast and let rest until mixture is frothy, about 10 minutes. In a large bowl, stir together flour, oil and salt, then pour in yeast mixture and knead into a smooth dough, about 3 to 4 minutes. Cover with plastic wrap and let rise at warm room temperature until doubled in size, about 1 hour.

3. While dough rises, place a pizza stone in the bottom of a cold oven and preheat oven to 500°F (260°C).

Prepare the Morel and Fiddlehead Topping
4. In a large skillet over medium-high heat, heat olive oil and butter until butter starts to bubble. Add shallots and morels and cook until morels have softened, about 2 minutes. Add fiddleheads and thyme and cook for 2 minutes more. Season to taste with salt and pepper and remove from heat.

Assemble and Bake the Pizzas
5. Punch down dough and divide into 6 equal pieces. Shape each piece into a ball. On a lightly floured surface, roll out 1 ball of dough into a 10-inch (25 cm) circle, ¼ inch (5 mm) thick. Sprinkle cornmeal onto pizza peel (or underside of a baking sheet) and place dough on the peel. Shake the peel to test that the dough will easily slide onto the pizza stone.

6. Brush rim of pizza with olive oil. Spread 1 to 2 tablespoons (15 to 30 mL) Basil Ramp Pesto evenly over the pizza. Sprinkle morels and fiddleheads over pesto. Rip mozzarella into pieces with your hands and distribute evenly. Slide pizza onto the hot stone and bake for 12 to 15 minutes, until the crust is golden and crisp and the cheese is bubbly. Let rest for a minute before slicing, and repeat with the remaining dough.

Peameal on a bun brings back memories of Saturdays shopping at the St. Lawrence Market in Toronto, where your first stop is to buy a peameal sandwich before you start your morning shop. The aïoli on this sandwich is an incredible condiment. I love how the sweetness of the honey and the sharpness of the mustard combine to create this rich and creamy aïoli, a wonderful accompaniment to a variety of sandwiches and snacks.

PEAMEAL on a BUN with SPRING ONION PICKLE RELISH and HONEY MUSTARD AÏOLI

Serves 4

Honey Mustard Aïoli
Makes 1 cup (250 mL)

1 clove garlic, minced
¼ teaspoon (1 mL) salt
1 cup (250 mL) mayonnaise
2 tablespoons (30 mL) whole-grain
    mustard (I like Kozlik's Triple
    Crunch Mustard)
1 tablespoon (15 mL) lemon juice
1 tablespoon (15 mL) honey

Spring Onion Pickle Relish
Makes 1 cup (250 mL)

6 slices maple bacon, diced
½ cup (125 mL) finely diced celery
    heart
¼ cup (60 mL) finely diced spring
    onions or green onions
1 small red chili, seeded and chopped
¼ cup (60 mL) finely diced dill pickle
2 tablespoons (30 mL) white wine
    vinegar
Kosher salt and cracked black pepper
2 tablespoons (30 mL) chopped celery
    leaves
2 tablespoons (30 mL) chopped
    flat-leaf parsley

Peameal Sandwiches
¼ cup (60 mL) honey
¼ cup (60 mL) Dijon mustard
1 pound (450 g) peameal bacon,
    thickly sliced into 16 slices
4 kaiser rolls
4 butter lettuce leaves

Make the Honey Mustard Aïoli

1. In a small bowl, stir together garlic, salt, mayonnaise, mustard, lemon juice and honey. Keep refrigerated for up to 1 week.

Make the Spring Onion Pickle Relish

2. In a sauté pan over medium heat, cook maple bacon until crisp. Add celery hearts, spring onions and chili; toss together. Then add pickles and vinegar and season with salt and pepper. Remove from heat and stir in celery leaves and parsley.

Prepare the Sandwiches

3. In a small bowl, whisk together honey and mustard. Heat a large skillet over medium-high heat. Add 4 slices bacon and brush tops with honey mustard glaze to coat well. Turn and brush with more glaze. Cook bacon until golden brown and cooked through, 1 to 2 minutes per side. Remove bacon to a plate and repeat with remaining bacon.

4. Cut rolls in half. Spread 1 tablespoon (15 mL) Honey Mustard Aïoli on the bottom half of the roll. Layer each sandwich with a lettuce leaf and 4 slices peameal bacon. Finish each sandwich with a large spoonful of Spring Onion Pickle Relish.

This steak is truly one of my favourites. Cooked to medium-rare perfection and served with bright, sharp chimichurri, there's no better way to eat steak in the spring! I always have a jar of this incredible chimichurri sauce in my fridge at home and at Ruby Watchco. It is one of the quickest sauces you can make, it's packed with flavour and goes so well on absolutely everything.

T-BONE STEAK with SPRING ONION CHIMICHURRI

Make the Spring Onion Chimichurri

1. Combine parsley, cilantro, vinegar, paprika, chili, thyme, spring onions and garlic in a small food processor and pulse until coarsely chopped. Add olive oil, season with salt and pepper and mix well with a spoon. Sauce can be stored tightly covered in the refrigerator for up to 1 week.

Prepare the T-Bone Steak

2. Remove steak from the refrigerator 1 hour before cooking. Preheat oven to 400°F (200°C).

3. In a large cast-iron pan, heat canola oil until shimmering. Season each side of steak with salt and pepper.

4. Place steak in the hot pan and sear on one side for about 3 minutes, then flip it over and sear on other side for 3 minutes more. Transfer the pan to the oven and continue to cook for 5 to 6 minutes or until internal temperature reaches 125°F (50°C).

5. Return pan to stove over high heat. Add butter, garlic, shishito peppers, rosemary and thyme. Baste steaks with melted butter for about 1 minute on each side.

6. When steak is cooked to your liking—130 to 135°F (55 to 58°C) for medium-rare, 140°F (60°C) for medium—remove it to a warm serving plate and let rest for about 10 minutes. Set aside pan with peppers and garlic.

7. Cut the steaks off the bone, then slice the meat across the grain. Top with shishito peppers, garlic and Spring Onion Chimichurri. Sprinkle with flaky sea salt and serve.

Serves 4

Spring Onion Chimichurri
Makes about 2 cups (500 mL)

1 cup (250 mL) flat-leaf parsley leaves
1 cup (250 mL) cilantro
½ cup (125 mL) red wine vinegar
1 teaspoon (5 mL) smoked paprika
1 teaspoon (5 mL) minced serrano chili
1 sprig thyme, leaves only
2 small spring onions
4 cloves garlic, peeled
½ cup (125 mL) extra-virgin olive oil
½ teaspoon (2 mL) kosher salt
¼ teaspoon (1 mL) cracked black
   pepper

T-Bone Steak

1 T-bone steak (about 2 pounds/900 g
   and 1½ to 2 inches/4 to 5 cm thick)
2 tablespoons (30 mL) canola oil
Kosher salt and coarsely ground black
   pepper
¼ cup (60 mL) unsalted butter
2 cloves garlic, crushed
1 cup (250 mL) shishito peppers
2 sprigs rosemary
2 sprigs thyme
Flaky sea salt

Ramps are intensely vibrant, with an incredible flavour profile—garlic, sweet onions and leeks all wrapped into one. Their growing season is very short, so I needed to figure out a way to hold on to those special flavours for as long as I could. Pickling was one of my first attempts at preserving ramps, and I've been using this recipe ever since. I have been known to add these to my Caesars, other salads and salsas. Highly recommended!

PICKLED RAMPS

Makes two 1-quart (1 L) jars

1 pound (450 g) ramps
4 tablespoons (60 mL) kosher salt, divided
1 cup (250 mL) granulated sugar
1 cup (250 mL) white wine vinegar
1 cup (250 mL) white wine
1 cup (250 mL) water
2 bay leaves
1 teaspoon (5 mL) mustard seeds
1 teaspoon (5 mL) coriander seeds
1 teaspoon (5 mL) fennel seeds
1 teaspoon (5 mL) pink peppercorns
1 teaspoon (5 mL) black peppercorns
1 teaspoon (5 mL) red pepper flakes

1. Trim root ends off ramps and cut off leaves, saving them for another use (like Ramp Butter on page 204). Rinse bulbs well under cool running water.

2. Bring a large pot of water to a boil and add 2 tablespoons (30 mL) salt. Drop in ramps and cook for 2 to 4 minutes, until tender. Transfer to a bowl of ice water until cool. Drain ramps well, then divide them between two 1-quart (1 L) mason jars.

3. In a saucepan, combine sugar, vinegar, white wine, water and remaining 2 tablespoons (30 mL) salt. Bring to a boil. Add bay leaves, mustard seeds, coriander, fennel, pink and black peppercorns and red pepper flakes.

4. Pour hot vinegar mixture over the ramps and let cool. Once cool, seal tightly and transfer to the refrigerator to pickle overnight. Use within 3 weeks.

STRAWBERRIES

When I think about strawberry season, it makes me very happy. I've spent my share of sunny afternoons at pick-your-own farms snacking my way through juicy handfuls, still warm and perfumed, each berry the perfect sweet mouthful. At the first sight of local strawberries in the farmers' markets—tiny and fragrant, bright red all the way through—I start imagining all the different ways to enjoy them. The simplest, and best, of course, is in a giant bowl topped with whipped cream. But I also love serving them in my Lemon-Strawberry Doughnuts with Vanilla Cream or incorporated in my Strawberry Ice Cream Sandwiches. I love baking with them, especially in my sweet-tart Strawberry Rhubarb Crisp with Pecan Crumble.

I just love the phrase "It's time to make the doughnuts!" So let's make the doughnuts. Yes, they may take a bit of time, but they are so worth the wait. You can make the vanilla pastry cream a couple of days ahead to speed up preparation. I always keep a big batch of pastry cream handy in my refrigerator during strawberry season, ready to make a whole slew of quick and delicious desserts.

LEMON-STRAWBERRY DOUGHNUTS with VANILLA CREAM

Makes about 12 doughnuts

Make the Vanilla Pastry Cream

1. In a medium saucepan, combine cream, milk, 2 tablespoons (30 mL) sugar and salt. Warm gently over medium-high heat, stirring to dissolve the sugar.

2. In a heatproof bowl, whisk egg yolks with remaining 2 tablespoons (30 mL) sugar until just mixed. In a small bowl, stir together cornstarch and water, then whisk cornstarch mixture into yolks. Slowly whisk about half of the warm cream mixture into the yolk mixture, whisking constantly to prevent lumps. Scrape yolk mixture back into remaining cream mixture. Cook, stirring constantly, until custard is thickened, about 3 minutes. Remove from heat and stir in vanilla and butter until melted.

3. Pour pastry cream through a medium-mesh sieve into a bowl. Press a piece of plastic wrap on top of the custard and let cool. Refrigerate until ready to use. The pastry cream can be kept in the refrigerator, covered, for up to 3 days.

Make the Doughnuts

4. In a stand mixer fitted with the paddle attachment, stir together 2 cups (500 mL) flour, yeast, 3 tablespoons (45 mL) sugar and salt. Add warm milk, vanilla and egg yolks. Mix on slow speed until smooth. Add remaining ¾ cup (175 mL) flour and the butter and mix on slow speed until incorporated. Continue to mix on medium speed until dough is soft, smooth and slightly sticky.

5. Cover bowl with plastic wrap and allow to rise for 1 hour, or refrigerate for up to 12 hours.

6. Dust a work surface with flour and turn out the dough. Using a lightly floured rolling pin, roll dough out to about ¼-inch (5 mm) thickness. Using a 3-inch (8 cm) round cutter, cut out 12 circles and place on a lightly floured baking sheet. Reroll the scraps and continue cutting out circles until you've used all the dough. Cover rounds with plastic wrap and let rise for about 30 minutes.

7. While doughnuts rise, in a large, deep pot, heat at least 2 inches (5 cm) oil to 360°F (185°C). Set a wire rack over paper towel.

Vanilla Pastry Cream
Makes about 1 cup (250 mL)
½ cup (125 mL) heavy (35%) cream
½ cup (125 mL) whole milk
4 tablespoons (60 mL) granulated sugar, divided
Pinch of salt
3 large egg yolks
2 tablespoons (30 mL) cornstarch
2 tablespoons (30 mL) water
1 teaspoon (5 mL) pure vanilla extract
2 tablespoons (30 mL) cold unsalted butter, cut into pieces

Doughnuts
2¾ cups (675 mL) bread flour, divided
1 packet (¼ ounce/7 g) instant yeast
3 tablespoons (45 mL) granulated sugar, plus ¼ cup (60 mL) for dusting
½ teaspoon (2 mL) salt
1 cup (250 mL) whole milk, warmed to 115°F (46°C)
1½ teaspoons (7 mL) pure vanilla extract
3 large egg yolks
¼ cup (60 mL) unsalted butter, at room temperature
Vegetable oil, for frying

To Serve
2 cups (500 mL) sliced hulled strawberries
Grated lemon zest
½ teaspoon (2 mL) pure vanilla extract
Icing sugar, for dusting

(Recipe continues)

8. Using a spatula, carefully lower a few doughnuts into the oil; do not crowd the pot. Fry for 1 to 2 minutes per side, turning a few times, until doughnuts are a light golden brown and cooked through. Remove with a spider or slotted spoon and drain on the wire rack. Return oil to 360°F (185°C) and repeat with remaining doughnuts. Let cool slightly before tossing in the remaining ¼ cup (60 mL) sugar. Let cool completely.

Prepare the Strawberries

9. While the doughnuts are cooling, toss strawberries with lemon zest and vanilla. Let strawberries sit for 15 minutes to allow flavours to develop.

Assemble the Doughnuts

10. Cut doughnuts in half crosswise. Spoon Vanilla Pastry Cream on the bottom half of each doughnut, then place a layer of sliced strawberries on top of the pastry cream. Top with the other half of the doughnut and sprinkle with icing sugar.

I have to thank June, my mother-in-law, for the best shortbread recipe. It's simple to prepare and the perfect cookie to hug a big scoop of strawberry ice cream.

STRAWBERRY ICE CREAM SANDWICHES

Makes 6 ice cream sandwiches

Strawberry Ice Cream
Makes about 6 cups (1.5 L)

2 cups (500 mL) strawberries, hulled and quartered

1 tablespoon (15 mL) lemon juice

1 cup (250 mL) granulated sugar, divided

4 large egg yolks

¼ teaspoon (1 mL) kosher salt

1½ cups (375 mL) whole milk

1½ cups (375 mL) heavy (35%) cream

1 vanilla bean, split lengthwise and seeds scraped out

June's Shortbread Cookies
Makes 12 cookies

1 cup (250 mL) cold unsalted butter

⅓ cup plus 2 tablespoons (105 mL) granulated sugar, plus more for sprinkling

2 cups (500 mL) all-purpose flour

½ cup (125 mL) cornstarch

¼ teaspoon (1 mL) salt

Make the Strawberry Ice Cream

1. In a medium bowl, combine strawberries, lemon juice and ¼ cup (60 mL) sugar. Toss until the sugar begins to dissolve. Let sit at room temperature for 30 minutes while you prepare the custard.

2. In a large bowl, whisk together egg yolks, the remaining ¾ cup (175 mL) sugar and salt until eggs look pale yellow and are well combined with the sugar. In a large saucepan over medium heat, bring milk, cream and vanilla seeds to a simmer. Whisking constantly, add a few ladles of the hot milk mixture to the yolk mixture. Whisk yolk mixture into remaining milk mixture. Reduce heat to low and cook, stirring constantly, until custard has thickened enough to coat the back of a wooden spoon, 4 to 6 minutes. Strain mixture into a bowl and set over another large bowl filled with ice water. Stir occasionally to cool, about 30 minutes.

3. Coarsely pulse half the strawberries and their juices in a food processor. Stir the chunky purée and remaining strawberries into the custard. Place in the refrigerator to continue to chill for at least 2 hours. You want the custard to be ice cold before churning.

4. Pour cold custard mixture into an ice cream maker and process according to the manufacturer's instructions until ice cream looks like thick soft serve. Scrape into an airtight container and freeze until hard, about 4 hours.

Make June's Shortbread Cookies

5. Preheat oven to 350°F (180°C).

6. In a stand mixer fitted with the paddle attachment, mix together butter and sugar until creamed, about 2 minutes. In a medium bowl, sift together flour, cornstarch and salt. Add flour mixture to creamed butter. Mix on low speed until dough starts to come together. Dump onto a flour-dusted surface and shape into a flat disc about 1 inch (2.5 cm) thick. Wrap in plastic wrap and refrigerate for 30 minutes, until firm but still pliable.

7. On a lightly floured surface, roll dough out to ½-inch (1 cm) thickness. Cut out cookies with a 2½-inch (6 cm) round cutter. Place cookies on an ungreased baking sheet and sprinkle with sugar. Bake for 15 to 20 minutes, until the edges begin to brown. Transfer to wire racks and allow to cool completely.

Assemble the Ice Cream Sandwiches

8. Sandwich a generous scoop of Strawberry Ice Cream between two of June's Shortbread Cookies and gently press together. These can be made ahead of time, wrapped in parchment paper and kept in the freezer until ready to eat. They will keep in the freezer for about 2 weeks.

This is not a complicated recipe at all, I know, but I love its simplicity, and I make this crisp at home all the time when this fruit combination is in season. Sweet, juicy strawberries and lip-puckering rhubarb topped with a buttery pecan crumble, this is a wonderfully comforting dessert and the perfect treat to lead us into summer! Serve warm with vanilla ice cream, or your own homemade Strawberry Ice Cream (see page 234).

STRAWBERRY RHUBARB CRISP with PECAN CRUMBLE

1. Preheat oven to 350°F (180°C).

2. In a large bowl, combine strawberries, rhubarb, granulated sugar, cornstarch and vanilla. Stir together well, then let sit at room temperature for 15 minutes. Pour mixture into an 11- × 9-inch (2.5 L) baking dish.

3. In a large bowl, combine brown sugar, graham cracker crumbs, flour, oats, pecans and salt. Add butter and 2 tablespoons (30 mL) water and mix everything together with your hands, creating a crumbly texture with a few large clumps.

4. Spread pecan crumble topping over fruit. Bake for 35 to 40 minutes or until the fruit is bubbling and the topping is golden brown.

Serves 6 to 8

4 cups (1 L) strawberries, hulled and halved

4 cups (1 L) rhubarb cut into 1-inch (2.5 cm) pieces

1 to 1¼ cups (250 to 300 mL) granulated sugar

2 tablespoons (30 mL) cornstarch

2 teaspoons (10 mL) pure vanilla extract

1 cup (250 mL) dark brown sugar

½ cup (125 mL) graham cracker crumbs

½ cup (125 mL) all-purpose flour

½ cup (125 mL) old-fashioned rolled oats

¼ cup (60 mL) pecans, toasted and chopped

½ teaspoon (2 mL) salt

¾ cup (175 mL) unsalted butter, cut into small dice

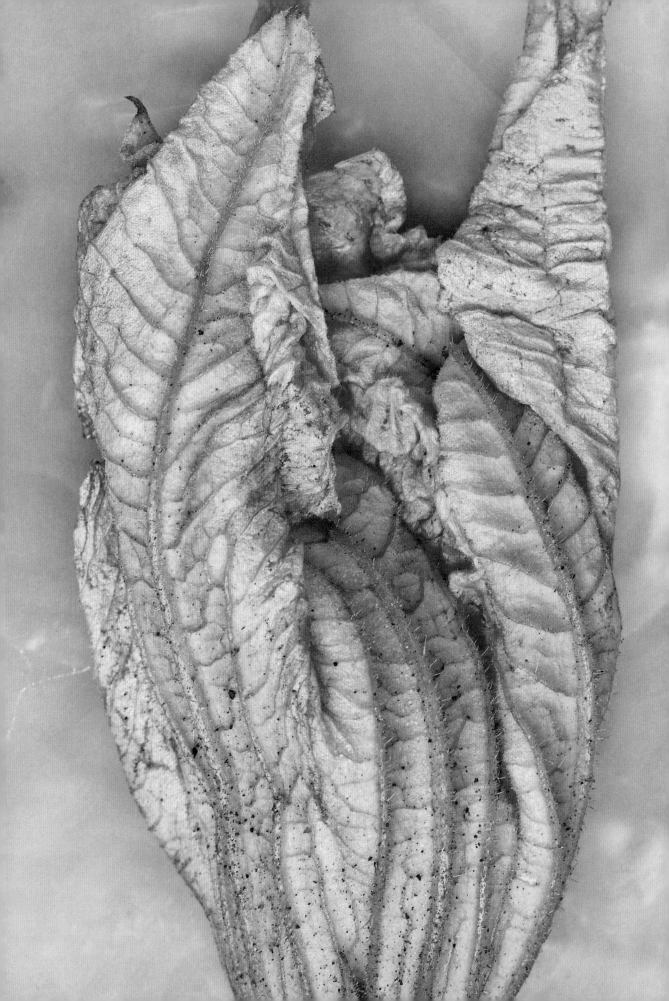

Beans
Berries
Cherries
Corn
Cucumbers
Eggplant
Fennel
Melons
Stone Fruits
Tomatoes
Zucchini and Summer Squash

Summer

BEANS

It's always a beautiful sight when the bushels of green, yellow and purple beans arrive at the market, long and slender with a brilliant snap to them. You'll find me preparing these beauties in all manner of ways, all summer long. So many delicious possibilities! Simple and raw for a quick snack; crisp-tender and dressed in a bright mustard vinaigrette in my Green Bean Niçoise Salad; or how about in an unusual yet perfect pairing with juicy summer fruit in my Summer Bean Salad with Peaches, Almonds and Pickled Blackberry Vinaigrette. With their neutral flavour profile, beans are the perfect canvas for stronger spices, garlic, mustard and bacon, or served simply with butter and a sprinkle of sea salt.

In my vegetarian version of the classic Niçoise salad, I put the focus on the wonderful summer green beans. Of course you could also use yellow beans, or a combination of both. For the vinaigrette I like to use Kozlik's Triple Crunch Mustard, but you could substitute your favourite mustard to make this dressing more your own.

GREEN BEAN NIÇOISE SALAD with MUSTARD VINAIGRETTE

1. In a saucepan of boiling salted water, cook beans for 2 minutes, then use a spider or large slotted spoon (do not drain the water) to transfer them to a bowl of ice water to stop the cooking process. Drain beans and pat dry with paper towel.

2. Return water to a boil, add eggs and cook for 7 minutes, then transfer to a bowl of ice water to stop the cooking process. Once cool, peel and halve eggs lengthwise.

3. In a large bowl, whisk together vinegar and mustard, then drizzle in oil, whisking until blended. Add beans, cherry tomatoes and olives and toss in the vinaigrette. Season well with salt and pepper.

4. Place mixed greens on a serving platter, then top with dressed bean mixture and egg halves yolk side up. Sprinkle with almonds and chervil.

Serves 4

1 pound (450 g) green beans, trimmed
4 large eggs
3 tablespoons (45 mL) rice vinegar
1 tablespoon (15 mL) whole-grain mustard
¼ cup (60 mL) canola oil
1 cup (250 mL) halved cherry tomatoes
¼ cup (60 mL) pitted Kalamata olives, halved lengthwise
Kosher salt and cracked black pepper
4 cups (1 L) mixed greens
3 tablespoons (45 mL) toasted sliced almonds
2 tablespoons (30 mL) chopped chervil

This terrific summer salad uses both fresh and pickled fruit, packing this dish with wonderful bite. I love the warm vinaigrette for this dish, and I think you will too! It starts to wilt the lettuce a tiny bit, creating different textures and flavours all on the same piece of lettuce.

SUMMER BEAN SALAD with PEACHES, ALMONDS and PICKLED BLACKBERRY VINAIGRETTE

Serves 4

½ pound (225 g) green beans
½ pound (225 g) yellow beans
2 heads Little Gem lettuce, leaves torn
4 thick slices bacon (6 ounces/170 g), finely diced
1 teaspoon (5 mL) chopped shallot
2 tablespoons (30 mL) pickling liquid from Pickled Blackberries (page 256)
1 teaspoon (5 mL) Dijon mustard
½ teaspoon (2 mL) honey
¼ cup (60 mL) Pickled Blackberries (page 256)
2 tablespoons (30 mL) extra-virgin olive oil
Kosher salt and cracked black pepper
3 peaches, pitted and cut into ½-inch (1 cm) wedges
2 tablespoons (30 mL) toasted sliced almonds
3 sprigs mint, leaves only

1. In a saucepan of boiling salted water, cook green and yellow beans until fork-tender, about 5 minutes. Drain beans and transfer to a bowl of ice water to stop the cooking process. Drain again, pat dry with paper towel and transfer to a large salad bowl. Add lettuce leaves.

2. In a large skillet, fry bacon over medium-high heat until brown and crisp. Using a slotted spoon, transfer bacon to paper towel to drain.

3. Add shallots to hot bacon fat and reduce heat to low. Add pickling liquid, mustard and honey and whisk to combine. Add pickled blackberries and oil.

4. Pour warm dressing over salad, season to taste with salt and pepper and toss gently. Arrange salad on a serving platter. Top with peaches and sprinkle over reserved bacon, almonds and mint.

BERRIES

Does anyone else do a happy dance when they see baskets of raspberries, blueberries and blackberries at the local market? I know I do! Never mind the candy-like snacking to follow, it means that summer is officially here. I love the sweet-tart, ruby-coloured pop of fresh raspberries and the juicy clean tang of plump blueberries. I've recently come around to the charms of the underrated blackberry too, with its deep, inky colour and almost winey sweetness. To celebrate, I'm sharing some of my most refreshing berry cocktail recipes— Electric Raspberry Lemonade and a Blueberry Mojito—as well as a few cottage dessert staples: my simple yet versatile Berry Galette, an Angel Food Cake with Berries and Sweet Cream and an amazing Blueberry Lemon Meringue Pie.

I love this summery cocktail. It's a fizzy concoction of mint, lime, rum and pomegranate blueberry juice. It's a little sweet, a little tart, and totally refreshing. If I had to choose, this would be my cocktail of the summer!

BLUEBERRY MOJITO

1. In a cocktail shaker, muddle mint, blueberries, and simple syrup. Add ice, rum, pomegranate blueberry juice and lime juice. Shake vigorously.

2. Strain into an ice-filled highball glass and top up with club soda. Garnish with whole blueberries, orange zest and mint.

Serves 1

6 to 8 fresh mint leaves
¼ cup (60 mL) blueberries
1 tablespoon (15 mL) Simple Syrup
   (see page 309)
1½ ounces (45 mL) white rum
½ cup (125 mL) pomegranate
   blueberry juice
2 tablespoons (30 mL) lime juice
¼ cup (60 mL) club soda
Whole blueberries, for garnish
1 strip orange zest, for garnish
Small mint sprig, for garnish

Nothing beats a chilled glass of lemonade on a hot summer day. I remember the fun as a kid hosting a lemonade stand on the sidewalk in front of our house. These days, I like to jazz up the lemonade with raspberries and vodka. Seems I've perfected this recipe over the years!

ELECTRIC RASPBERRY LEMONADE

Make the Raspberry Simple Syrup

1. Heat water in a small pan on the stove until almost boiling. Add the sugar and stir to dissolve. Cool slightly, then pour into a blender along with the raspberries and pulse until puréed. Pour the simple syrup through a fine-mesh sieve to strain out the seeds. Cool in refrigerator.

Prepare the Electric Raspberry Lemonade

2. In a medium pitcher, combine the Raspberry Simple Syrup, water, lemon juice and vodka. Pour raspberry lemonade into ice-filled glasses. Garnish with mint, raspberries and lemon slices, if using.

Serves 4

Raspberry Simple Syrup

1½ cups (375 mL) water
½ cup (125 mL) granulated sugar
2 cups (500 mL) raspberries

Electric Raspberry Lemonade

1½ cups (375 mL) water
½ to ¾ cup (125 to 175 mL) freshly
     squeezed lemon juice
6 ounces (175 mL) raspberry vodka

For Assembly

Small mint sprigs, for garnish
Raspberries, for garnish
Lemon slices, for garnish, if desired

This is one of my favourite desserts to make when I have fresh summer berries handy. Angel food cake is delicate, airy, melts in your mouth and tastes like vanilla heaven. It is the ideal vessel to showcase sweet berries. This very simple but elegant dessert is the perfect ending to any meal.

ANGEL FOOD CAKE with BERRIES and SWEET CREAM

Serves 10 to 12

Angel Food Cake
1¼ cups (300 mL) sifted cake-and-pastry flour
1½ cups (375 mL) granulated sugar, divided
¼ teaspoon (1 mL) salt
1¾ cups (425 mL) egg whites (from 13 to 15 large eggs), at room temperature
1½ teaspoons (7 mL) cream of tartar
1 teaspoon (5 mL) pure vanilla extract

Sweet Whipped Cream
Makes about 2 cups (500 mL)
1 cup (250 mL) heavy (35%) cream
1 to 2 tablespoons (15 to 30 mL) granulated sugar, to taste
1 teaspoon (5 mL) pure vanilla extract

For Assembly
2 cups (500 mL) assorted summer berries, such as blackberries, raspberries, blueberries and strawberries

Make the Angel Food Cake
1. Preheat oven to 350°F (180°C). Grease a nonstick 10-inch (25 cm) tube pan.

2. Stir together flour, ¾ cup (175 mL) sugar and salt in a medium bowl until well mixed; set aside.

3. In a large bowl, beat egg whites with an electric mixer on low speed until frothy. Add cream of tartar and beat on high speed until soft peaks form. Gradually beat in remaining ¾ cup (175 mL) sugar, about 2 tablespoons (30 mL) at a time. Beat until sugar is dissolved, mixture is glossy and stiff peaks form, then beat in vanilla. Sift flour mixture over egg white mixture in 4 parts, gently folding until just blended after each addition.

4. Pour batter into prepared tube pan. Smooth top, then run a knife through the batter to break up any air pockets. Bake until cake is golden brown and top springs back when gently pressed, 30 to 40 minutes. Set cake pan upside down on a wire rack to cool completely.

Make the Sweet Whipped Cream
5. In a large, deep bowl, beat heavy cream until soft peaks form. Sprinkle 1 to 2 tablespoons (15 to 30 mL) granulated sugar over cream. Beat until soft peaks return, then beat in vanilla.

Assemble the Cake
6. Run a thin knife around side of pan to loosen the cooled cake. Invert cake onto a serving plate. Serve cake with berries and Sweet Whipped Cream.

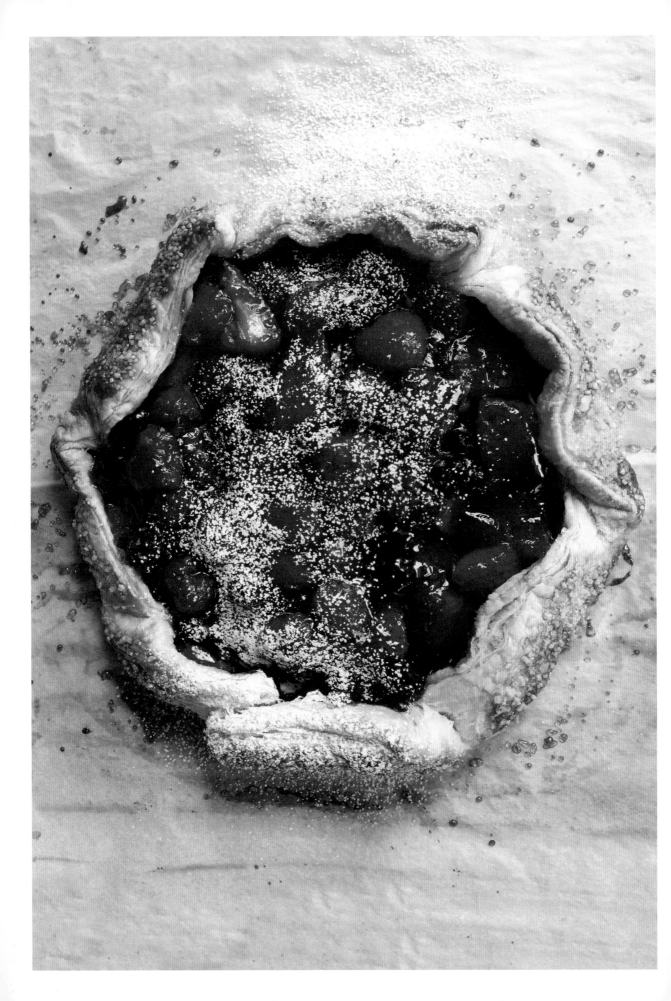

This is a perfect recipe if you're just starting out in baking or a fun one to make with kids because galettes are free-form and rustic. I love the simplicity of a galette—it's really just a beautiful buttery crust holding a delicious juicy, jam-like fruit filling. Another great thing about galettes is that you will never be judged on their presentation—especially if you pack in as many different berries as you can!

BERRY GALETTE

Make the Galette Dough

1. In a food processor, combine flour, sugar, salt, butter and shortening. Pulse into pea-size crumbles. Add water, a few tablespoons at a time, and pulse until dough comes together and all the water has been added. Divide dough in half and flatten each half into a disc. Wrap discs in plastic wrap and chill 1 disc in the refrigerator for at least 1 hour before using. The second disc can be used the next time you make a galette, and can be stored in the freezer for up to 2 months.

2. Preheat oven to 350°F (180°C) and line a large baking sheet with parchment paper.

Prepare the Berry Filling

3. In a medium bowl, toss berries with sugar and cornstarch.

Assemble and Bake the Galette

4. Lightly flour a work surface and roll out dough to a 12-inch (30 cm) round. Transfer to the prepared baking sheet. Spoon berry filling into the centre of the dough, leaving a border about 1½ inches (4 cm) around the edge. Fold the edge of the dough over the fruit, making occasional pleats to hold it in place. Brush dough with cream. Sprinkle Demerara sugar evenly over dough and fruit.

5. Bake galette until the crust is light brown and the filling bubbles, about 50 minutes. Let cool for at least 10 minutes and dust with icing sugar before serving.

Serves 4 to 6

Galette Dough
3 cups (750 mL) all-purpose flour
2 tablespoons (30 mL) granulated sugar
1 teaspoon (5 mL) salt
¾ cup (175 mL) cold unsalted butter, cut into chunks
⅓ cup (75 mL) cold vegetable shortening, cut into chunks
6 to 8 tablespoons (90 to 125 mL) cold water

Berry Filling
2 cups (500 mL) mixed berries, such as blackberries, raspberries, blueberries and strawberries
½ cup (125 mL) granulated sugar
1 tablespoon (15 mL) cornstarch

For Assembly
1 tablespoon (15 mL) heavy (35%) cream
2 tablespoons (30 mL) Demerara sugar

To Serve
Icing sugar, for dusting

Lemon meringue pie is a classic, with that tart lemon filling and airy meringue. I've added summer blueberries to take this pie to the next level. Of course you could always use another berry, like raspberries or blackberries.

BLUEBERRY LEMON MERINGUE PIE

Serves 8 to 10

Sweet Pastry Dough
1¼ cups (300 mL) all-purpose flour
½ cup (125 mL) icing sugar
¼ teaspoon (1 mL) salt
½ cup (125 mL) cold unsalted butter, cut into chunks
2 large egg yolks, lightly beaten

Lemon Filling
1¼ cups (300 mL) granulated sugar
6 tablespoons (90 mL) cornstarch
1 cup (250 mL) whole milk
⅛ teaspoon (0.5 mL) salt
2 tablespoons (30 mL) grated lemon zest
½ cup (125 mL) freshly squeezed lemon juice
6 large egg yolks (reserve egg whites for meringue)
3 tablespoons (45 mL) cold unsalted butter, cut into 3 pieces

Blueberry Sauce
1 cup (250 mL) blueberries
2 tablespoons (30 mL) granulated sugar
Grated zest and juice of 1 orange
3 tablespoons (45 mL) cornstarch

Meringue
6 large egg whites, at room temperature
½ cup (125 mL) granulated sugar
½ teaspoon (2 mL) cream of tartar

Prepare and Blind Bake the Sweet Pastry Dough

1. Preheat oven to 350°F (180°C). In a medium bowl, combine flour, icing sugar and salt. Using your fingertips, cut butter into dry ingredients until mixture resembles pea-size crumbles. Add egg yolks, and gently rub mixture together. The dough should come together quickly and feel moist and crumbly. Dust your fingers with flour and press dough evenly over the bottom and sides of a 9-inch (23 cm) tart pan with a removable bottom. Wrap completely with plastic wrap and chill in the refrigerator for 30 minutes.

2. Line pie shell with a large piece of parchment paper and fill it with pie weights. Place on a baking sheet and bake for 12 to 15 minutes, until edges are just starting to turn golden. Remove parchment paper and pie weights and bake for another 5 to 7 minutes, until the bottom is lightly golden. Allow pie shell to cool completely on a wire rack.

Make the Lemon Filling

3. Combine sugar, cornstarch, milk, and salt in a large nonreactive saucepan. Whisk to combine. Bring to a simmer over medium heat, whisking occasionally, and simmer for 3 to 4 minutes or until sauce has thickened. Whisk in lemon zest and juice. Remove sauce from heat.

4. In a medium bowl, gradually whisk about 1 cup (250 mL) sauce into egg yolks, then whisk yolk mixture into remaining sauce. Continue to cook, whisking constantly for 2 to 3 minutes, until filling is thick and glossy. Remove from heat and whisk in butter, 1 piece at a time.

5. Pour Lemon Filling into baked pie shell, smoothing the top. Allow to cool.

Make the Blueberry Sauce

6. While the filling is cooling in the pie shell, in a medium saucepan, combine blueberries, sugar, orange zest and half of the orange juice. Cook over medium heat for about 5 minutes, until blueberries begin to boil. Stir cornstarch into remaining orange juice, then stir cornstarch mixture into the sauce. Cook, stirring, until sauce thickens. Remove from heat and allow to cool.

7. Preheat oven to 400°F (200°C).

Make the Meringue

8. In a large bowl, beat egg whites with an electric mixer on high speed until foamy. Gradually beat in sugar and cream of tartar until stiff peaks form.

Assemble and Bake the Pie

9. Spoon Blueberry Sauce over cooled filling, then spread meringue over sauce, making peaks with the back of a spoon.

10. Bake pie until meringue is golden brown, 15 to 20 minutes. Cool on a wire rack to room temperature, about 30 minutes. Refrigerate pie until completely chilled, about 3 hours, before serving.

When summer berries are in season I jump at the chance to pickle them, because I love the balance of sweet and sour. Raw blackberries tend to be a bit sour, but when cooked they turn sweet and jammy. Blackberries are precious little gems, and I want to enjoy them for as long as I can. Pickling is a wonderful way to do just that! You won't regret having these around in the colder months, when you can add them to a cheese plate, to cocktails or even to a rich sauce that would accompany a roast. In the summer, they are wonderful in my Summer Bean Salad with Peaches, Almonds and Pickled Blackberry Vinaigrette (page 244).

PICKLED BLACKBERRIES

Makes three 1-pint (500 mL) jars

1 shallot, quartered lengthwise
2½-inch (6 cm) cinnamon stick, broken in half
1-inch (2.5 cm) piece fresh ginger, peeled and thinly sliced
1 sprig thyme
1 small bay leaf
1½ cups (375 mL) white or red wine vinegar
1½ cups (375 mL) water
¾ cup (175 mL) granulated sugar
1 tablespoon (15 mL) salt
1 teaspoon (5 mL) mustard seeds
1 teaspoon (5 mL) black peppercorns
3 cups (750 mL) blackberries

1. In a medium saucepan, combine shallot, cinnamon, ginger, thyme, bay leaf, vinegar, water, sugar, salt, mustard seeds and peppercorns. Bring to a boil over medium heat, stirring to dissolve sugar and salt, and continue to simmer for 15 minutes. Let brine cool completely.

2. Strain pickling liquid and divide evenly into clean 1-pint (500 mL) jars. Add the blackberries. Seal and refrigerate for at least 1 week before serving. They will keep refrigerated for up to 1 month.

CHERRIES

Cherries may just be one of my favourite fruits. When it's bright and hot in the middle of summer, there is something positively luxurious about snacking on a bowlful of cherries. With so many different varieties available, it may just take you the entire summer to try them all! I'm a big fan of the popular Bing variety; it's the classic ruby-red cherry perfect for eating fresh. Vans are excellent for making a cobbler or preserves because of their sweet, firm texture and deep, rich colour. The bright yellow-and-blush Rainier cherries are delicate, super-sweet and almost creamy, and are a superb choice for my Cheesecake with Honey-Roasted Cherries.

When you have company for brunch, this recipe will wow the crowd. It's your basic French toast but with a summery twist—a brilliant brown butter cherry sauce that makes this version of French toast the best. I love it so much, I've been known to make this twice in one day, for brunch and for a late-night snack!

STUFFED FRENCH TOAST with BROWN BUTTER CHERRY SAUCE

Serves 4

Brown Butter Cherry Sauce

2 tablespoons (30 mL) unsalted butter
¼ cup (60 mL) dark brown sugar
1 vanilla bean, split lengthwise and seeds scraped out
2 cups (500 mL) pitted cherries

Cream Cheese Filling

1 package (8 ounces/225 g) cream cheese, softened
¼ cup (60 mL) mascarpone cheese, softened
¼ cup (60 mL) granulated sugar
¼ cup (60 mL) icing sugar, sifted
2 tablespoons (30 mL) lemon juice

French Toast

6 large eggs
1 cup (250 mL) heavy (35%) cream
2 teaspoons (10 mL) grated lemon zest
2 to 4 tablespoons (30 to 60 mL) unsalted butter
8 slices sweet challah bread (1 inch/2.5 cm thick)

To Serve

¼ cup (60 mL) toasted slivered almonds
¼ cup (60 mL) icing sugar, sifted

Make the Brown Butter Cherry Sauce

1. In a skillet over medium heat, melt butter and cook until foam subsides and butter is dark brown and smells nutty. Stir in brown sugar, vanilla seeds and cherries and cook until cherries have released their juices and are thoroughly heated, about 5 minutes. With a slotted spoon, transfer cherries to a bowl.

2. Reduce pan juices until thick enough to coat the back of a spoon, then stir into cherries. Keep sauce warm.

Prepare the Cream Cheese Filling

3. In a medium bowl, whisk together cream cheese, mascarpone, granulated sugar, icing sugar and lemon juice until blended.

Prepare the French Toast

4. In a medium bowl, whisk together eggs, cream and lemon zest.

5. Preheat oven to 325°F (160°C). Melt 2 tablespoons (30 mL) butter in a large skillet over medium heat. Working in batches, dip bread slices into egg mixture, coating both sides. Let excess egg mixture drip back into bowl. Place bread slices in skillet and fry until golden, adding more butter if necessary, about 3 minutes per side, turning only once. Transfer to a baking sheet and keep warm in oven.

6. Place 1 slice of French toast on each of 4 plates. Spoon over Cream Cheese Filling and place remaining French toast slice on top. Spoon over warm Brown Butter Cherry Sauce, garnish with almonds and icing sugar, and serve immediately.

A perfect dessert always involves a perfect combination. Cherries and cheesecake is one of those. This is a recipe I always return to, and I think you will too. The lemon and orange brighten the flavour of the cream cheese, and the cherry topping is so simple to make, but the secret is really in the honey. Buy a local unpasteurized variety—the flavour will amaze you. Make sure to plan ahead: you'll need to chill the cheesecake for at least 8 hours.

CHEESECAKE with HONEY-ROASTED CHERRIES

Make the Cheesecake

1. Preheat oven to 325°F (160°C) and grease a 9-inch (23 cm) springform pan.

2. In a medium bowl, stir together cookie crumbs and butter until combined. Press crumb mixture into bottom of springform pan. Place the pan on a baking sheet and bake for 8 to 12 minutes, until golden brown. Cool on a wire rack.

3. Preheat oven to 350°F (180°C).

4. In a stand mixer fitted with the paddle attachment, beat cream cheese, sugar, flour, orange and lemon zests and vanilla until blended.

5. Add eggs and yolks, 1 at a time, beating well after each addition. Add cream and beat until blended.

6. Pour filling over cooled crust and smooth top. Bake until just set and firm to the touch, about 1 hour. Transfer pan to a wire rack and let cool completely, then cover and refrigerate for at least 8 hours or overnight.

Make the Cherry Topping

7. While cheesecake is chilling, in a large saucepan over medium heat, cook honey until thickened, about 5 minutes. Add cherries and cook for 5 minutes more, stirring frequently.

8. Transfer cherry mixture to a bowl, cover and refrigerate until ready to serve. If necessary, strain accumulated liquid from cherries before topping cheesecake.

9. To serve, run a thin knife around cake edge before releasing springform ring. Serve cheesecake with Cherry Topping spooned over top.

Serves 10 to 12

Cheesecake
1¼ cups (300 mL) fine chocolate cookie crumbs
¼ cup (60 mL) unsalted butter, melted
5 packages (8 ounces/225 g each) cream cheese, softened
1¼ cups (300 mL) granulated sugar
3 tablespoons (45 mL) all-purpose flour
1 teaspoon (5 mL) grated orange zest
1 teaspoon (5 mL) grated lemon zest
½ teaspoon (2 mL) pure vanilla extract
5 large eggs
2 large egg yolks
¼ cup (60 mL) heavy (35%) cream

Cherry Topping
½ cup (125 mL) honey
2 cups (500 mL) pitted and halved cherries, such as Rainiers

CORN

Sweet corn is the quintessential taste of summer. I love driving to the cottage and stopping at the farmer's laneway, where there is a big wagon piled high with irresistible ears of corn. Just picked, it is the sweetest and most delicately flavoured. One of the simplest ways to serve corn is on the cob with butter—sweet and rich, they make the perfect couple. Or try spicing up the corn and butter combo with garlic, lime, chipotle, cilantro, mango or bacon with my Grilled Corn with Four Butters and turn it into the ultimate summer favourite. But why stop there? Corn's natural flavour pairs beautifully with smoky and bright additions too. You might have to jump back in your car and head back to the farmer's laneway for more!

Everyone loves grilled corn in the summer with lots of butter. My twist on this summer classic is whipping up a few different and fun butters to make the grilled corn shine. These ones are easy to make and full of flavour. The best part is you can make them ahead of time and pop them out of the fridge just as your corn is ready to be slathered in butter.

GRILLED CORN with FOUR BUTTERS

Grill the Corn

1. Preheat grill to high heat.

2. Bring a pot of salted water to a boil. Add corn and cook for 5 minutes. Remove with tongs.

3. Carefully oil the hot grill. Put corn on the grill, close lid and barbecue until nicely charred on all sides, about 6 to 8 minutes, turning often. Serve immediately with butters and garnishes, if using.

❶ Bacon Butter with Cheddar and Green Onions

Makes about 1 cup (250 mL)

½ cup (125 mL) unsalted butter, softened
½ cup (125 mL) grated aged cheddar cheese
6 slices bacon, cooked until crisp, finely chopped
4 green onions, finely chopped
½ teaspoon (2 mL) finely chopped thyme
½ teaspoon (2 mL) salt
⅛ teaspoon (0.5 mL) cracked black pepper
Additional cheddar cheese, bacon and green onions, for garnish, if desired

1. In a small bowl, stir together butter, cheddar, bacon, green onions, thyme, salt and pepper until combined. Cover and refrigerate until ready to serve.

❷ Chipotle Butter with Cotija Cheese

Makes about 1 cup (250 mL)

½ cup (125 mL) unsalted butter, softened
¼ cup (60 mL) crumbled cotija cheese
1 teaspoon (5 mL) adobo sauce, from a can of chipotles in adobo
1 teaspoon (5 mL) chili powder
1 teaspoon (5 mL) kosher salt
½ teaspoon (2 mL) ground cumin
½ teaspoon (2 mL) grated lime zest
1 tablespoon (15 mL) lime juice
Lime wedges, cilantro leaves and additional cotija cheese, for garnish, if desired

1. In a small bowl, stir together butter, cotija, adobo, chili powder, salt, cumin, lime zest and lime juice until combined. Cover and refrigerate until ready to serve.

Serves 4

4 sweet corn cobs, shucked
Vegetable oil, for grill

(Recipe continues)

❸ Mango Butter with Cayenne and Lime

Makes about 1 cup (250 mL)

½ cup (125 mL) unsalted butter, softened
½ cup (125 mL) finely diced mango
1 teaspoon (5 mL) minced peeled fresh ginger
½ teaspoon (2 mL) turmeric
½ teaspoon (2 mL) kosher salt
½ teaspoon (2 mL) grated lime zest
2 teaspoons (10 mL) lime juice
¼ teaspoon (1 mL) cayenne pepper
⅛ teaspoon (0.5 mL) cracked black pepper
Chopped chives and thinly sliced red chili, for garnish, if desired

1. In a small bowl, stir together butter, mango, ginger, turmeric, salt, lime zest, lime juice, cayenne and black pepper until combined. Cover and refrigerate until ready to serve.

❹ Garlic Herb Butter with Lemon and Parmesan

Makes about 1 cup (250 mL)

½ cup (125 mL) unsalted butter, softened
½ cup (125 mL) grated Parmesan cheese
¼ cup (60 mL) finely chopped flat-leaf parsley
1 clove garlic, minced
½ teaspoon (2 mL) grated lemon zest
1 teaspoon (5 mL) lemon juice
½ teaspoon (2 mL) kosher salt
⅛ teaspoon (0.5 mL) cracked black pepper
Chopped cherry tomatoes, basil leaves and additional Parmesan cheese, for garnish, if desired

1. In a small bowl, stir together butter, Parmesan, parsley, garlic, lemon zest, lemon juice, salt and pepper until combined. Cover and refrigerate until ready to serve.

This tender and sweet cornbread is the perfect accompaniment to any barbecue-style dish. I know that baking might seem a little ambitious at dinnertime, but rest assured, this cornbread is easy to make. You can serve it instead of a traditional starch, and leftovers—if there are any—are delicious for breakfast, warmed up and slathered with honey, butter or jam.

SUMMER CORNBREAD

Serves 8 to 10

1. Preheat oven to 425°F (220°C) and grease a 10-inch (25 cm) cast-iron skillet or a 2-quart (2 L) baking dish.

2. In a large bowl, stir together flour, cornmeal, sugar, baking powder and salt until blended. In a medium bowl, whisk together eggs, milk, oil, butter and corn kernels. Stir into dry ingredients until just combined.

3. Spoon batter into skillet or baking dish and bake until a toothpick inserted into centre comes out clean, about 20 minutes. Let cornbread cool in pan for 5 minutes, then carefully turn out onto wire rack and let cool completely.

2 cups (500 mL) all-purpose flour
1 cup (250 mL) cornmeal
¾ cup (175 mL) granulated sugar
1 tablespoon (15 mL) baking powder
½ teaspoon (2 mL) kosher salt
2 large eggs
1½ cups (375 mL) milk
1¼ cups (300 mL) vegetable oil
¼ cup (60 mL) unsalted butter, melted
1 cup (250 mL) sweet corn kernels

This is an impressive recipe to add to your collection for summer barbecue side dishes, but it's also the perfect meal if you just want to treat yourself. This creamy mac and cheese, studded with sweet summer corn and juicy lobster, really is the grown-up version of the childhood classic.

SWEET CORN and LOBSTER MAC and CHEESE

Serves 4

2 live lobsters (about 1¼ pounds/
   565 g each)
2 tablespoons (30 mL) unsalted butter
2 small shallots, minced
1 teaspoon (5 mL) chopped thyme
3 tablespoons (45 mL) all-purpose
   flour
1 cup (250 mL) heavy (35%) cream
2 cups (500 mL) whole milk
2 teaspoons (10 mL) Dijon mustard
2 cups (500 mL) sweet corn kernels
8 ounces (225 g) aged white cheddar
   cheese, grated
Kosher salt and cracked black pepper
12 ounces (340 g) macaroni
Chopped chives, for garnish

1. To cook the lobster, bring a large pot of salted water to a boil over high heat. Grasp lobster by the body and lower it head first into the boiling water. Cover the pot and bring back to a boil, then cook for 6 to 7 minutes. Remove lobsters with tongs and place in a colander in the sink; allow to cool. Remove meat from tail, claws and knuckles and coarsely chop.

2. In a large saucepan over medium heat, melt butter. Add shallots and thyme and cook until shallots are translucent, about 3 minutes, stirring often. Stir in flour and cook for 2 minutes more, stirring constantly.

3. Whisk in cream and milk and continue cooking until sauce is thick enough to coat the back of a spoon, 8 to 10 minutes.

4. Stir in mustard, sweet corn and cheddar until combined. Cook for 5 minutes, stirring constantly, until corn is cooked. Season to taste with salt and pepper. Cover and keep warm.

5. Bring another large pot of salted water to a boil over high heat. Cook macaroni according to package directions until al dente. Drain well. Fold pasta and lobster meat into sauce until combined. Spoon pasta into warmed bowls and serve garnished with chives.

This recipe screams summer to me, with the corn cooked two ways. It gives you the opportunity to have smoky charred corn salsa and sweet and silky creamed corn all in one dish. It's a perfect combination with the delicate white-fleshed pickerel. If you don't have pickerel on hand, this dish will taste equally delicious with your favourite fish, or chicken or steak.

PAN-SEARED PICKEREL with CHARRED and CREAMED CORN

Serves 4

Make the Creamed Corn

1. In a medium skillet over medium-high heat, heat olive oil. Add garlic and onion and sauté for 5 minutes.

2. Add butter, thyme and corn and sauté for about 5 minutes. Stir in cream and heat through. Remove from heat and discard thyme sprigs. Season to taste with salt and pepper and keep warm until ready to serve.

Make the Charred Corn

3. Preheat oven to 350°F (180°C) and line a baking sheet with parchment paper.

4. Toss cornbread cubes with 2 tablespoons (30 mL) oil until coated, then spread in a single layer on baking sheet. Bake until golden brown, about 15 minutes, tossing occasionally.

5. Meanwhile, in a skillet over medium heat, heat remaining 2 tablespoons (30 mL) oil. Add onion and sauté until translucent, about 5 minutes, stirring often. Stir in chili and garlic and cook for 1 minute more.

6. Scrape onion mixture into a large bowl. Add corn kernels, parsley, green onions and toasted cornbread cubes; toss gently to combine. Season to taste with salt and pepper.

Prepare the Pickerel

7. In a skillet over medium-high heat, heat oil. Pat fish dry and season with salt and pepper. Add fillets to skillet skin side down and fry until crisp and golden, about 2 minutes per side.

8. To serve, spoon Creamed Corn onto plates and top with fish. Spoon Charred Corn over fish and serve immediately.

Creamed Corn

1 tablespoon (15 mL) olive oil
2 cloves garlic, minced
1 small yellow onion, finely diced
3 tablespoons (45 mL) unsalted butter
2 sprigs thyme
2 cups (500 mL) coarsely grated sweet
    corn kernels (about 4 cobs)
½ cup (125 mL) heavy (35%) cream
Kosher salt and cracked black pepper

Charred Corn

2 cups (500 mL) Summer Cornbread
    (page 267) cut into 1-inch (2.5 cm)
    cubes
4 tablespoons (60 mL) olive oil,
    divided
½ cup (125 mL) finely diced red onion
1 teaspoon (5 mL) minced Fresno chili
1 clove garlic, minced
Kernels from 2 cobs grilled sweet corn
    (see page 263; about 1 cup/250 mL
    kernels)
½ cup (125 mL) chopped flat-leaf
    parsley leaves
2 green onions, thinly sliced on the
    diagonal
Kosher salt and cracked black pepper

Pickerel

2 tablespoons (30 mL) canola oil
4 skin-on pickerel fillets (about
    5 ounces/140 g each)
Kosher salt and cracked black pepper

I think right after potatoes, corn is my favourite vegetable, and it shines in this great summer side dish. The aged cheddar complements the sweet summer corn, and the jalapeño adds a wonderful heat to the succotash. If you are a fan of spice, you could switch out jalapeño for bird's-eye chilies or your favourite variety. On the same note, if you prefer things milder, then just leave it out. This is a great side dish to serve alongside barbecued chicken or grilled shrimp.

SWEET CORN SUCCOTASH

Serves 4

2 tablespoons (30 mL) canola oil
2 cups (500 mL) sweet corn kernels
1 cup (250 mL) diced zucchini
½ cup (125 mL) finely diced red onion
1 jalapeño pepper, seeded and finely
    diced
1 clove garlic, minced
1 cup (250 mL) shelled edamame
1 teaspoon (5 mL) My Old Bay
    Seasoning (see page 287) or
    store-bought
½ cup (125 mL) heavy (35%) cream
½ cup (125 mL) grated aged white
    cheddar cheese
Kosher salt and cracked black pepper
Basil leaves, for garnish, if desired

1. Heat oil in a large skillet over medium-high heat. Add corn, zucchini, onion, jalapeño and garlic and sauté until corn is tender, about 10 minutes, stirring occasionally.

2. Add edamame and old bay seasoning and sauté for 5 minutes more, stirring occasionally.

3. Stir in cream and cook until slightly thickened, about 3 minutes. Add cheddar and stir until cheese melts. Season to taste with salt and pepper, garnish with basil, if using, and serve.

CUCUMBERS

In a summer landscape full of loud and punchy personalities—the look-at-me of juicy berries and high-fiving flavour of ripe tomatoes and sweet corn—cucumbers provide a welcome and much-needed relief. Loaded with vitamins and minerals, cucumbers are 95 percent water, so it's no wonder they help rehydrate the body, get rid of bad breath, cure a hangover and aid digestion. They provide a refreshing crunch in big, bold Greek salads or a delicate flavour to chilled soups, like my Chilled Cucumber and Melon Gazpacho. I also love adding the fresh taste of cucumbers to cocktails. Trust me, there's nothing better than a Cucumber Gin Fizz on a hot summer night . . . and no hangover!

A gazpacho is a perfect way to turn those ripe melons and cucumbers into a refreshing soup. The mint and lime juice add a special brightness, resulting in a chilled soup that screams summer! This gazpacho is perfect as is, but go ahead and add grilled shrimp or scallops to the garnish for extra wow appeal.

CHILLED CUCUMBER and MELON GAZPACHO

Serves 6

Cucumber and Melon Gazpacho
4 cups (1 L) chopped honeydew melon flesh (about 1 medium melon)
2 cups (500 mL) seeded and diced English cucumber
¼ cup (60 mL) lime juice
2 tablespoons (30 mL) honey
2 sprigs mint, leaves only
Kosher salt and cracked black pepper

Honey-Lime Dressing
Makes about ¼ cup (60 mL)
2 tablespoons (30 mL) honey
2 tablespoons (30 mL) lime juice
4 mint leaves, very thinly sliced into ribbons
½ teaspoon (2 mL) minced serrano chili
Pinch of kosher salt

To Serve
2 mini cucumbers, thinly sliced into rounds
2 small radishes, thinly sliced into rounds
6 tablespoons (90 mL) sour cream

Make the Cucumber and Melon Gazpacho

1. In a food processor, combine melon, cucumber, lime juice, honey and mint leaves. Process until smooth. Transfer to a bowl and season to taste with salt and pepper. Cover and refrigerate for at least 3 hours to allow flavours to develop.

Make the Honey-Lime Dressing

2. While gazpacho is chilling, whisk together honey, lime juice, mint, chili and salt until combined. Cover and refrigerate until ready to serve.

3. To serve, ladle gazpacho into chilled soup bowls. Toss mini cucumber and radish rounds with Honey-Lime Dressing and place on top of soup along with a spoonful of sour cream.

Have a craving for some spicy barbecue wings but forgot to grab barbecue sauce? You have nothing to worry about with this recipe in your back pocket—chances are you already have these condiments in your fridge. This is an easy and tasty sauce for grilled chicken wings, chicken legs or steak. The Creamy Cucumber Old Bay Dip will be just what you need to balance out these spicy wings.

SPICY BARBECUE WINGS with CREAMY CUCUMBER OLD BAY DIP

Prepare the Spicy Barbecue Wings

1. Remove wing tips from chicken wings and save for stock or discard. Cut wings through the joint into flats and drumettes and place in a large bowl.

2. In a small bowl, whisk together Dijon and yellow mustards, Sriracha, Worcestershire sauce, oil, salt and pepper until blended. Add marinade to wings and toss to coat. Cover and refrigerate for 1 hour to allow flavours to meld.

Make the Creamy Cucumber Old Bay Dip

3. While chicken is marinating, in a small bowl, stir together cucumber, mayonnaise, sour cream, lemon juice, herbs and old bay seasoning until blended. Season to taste with salt and pepper. Cover and refrigerate until ready to serve.

Grill the Spicy Barbecue Wings

4. Preheat grill to medium heat.

5. Remove wings from marinade and grill, turning occasionally, until internal temperature reaches 165°F (74°C), about 20 minutes. Serve wings with a side of Creamy Cucumber Old Bay Dip and sliced cucumber.

Serves 4

Spicy Barbecue Wings

3 pounds (1.35 kg) chicken wings
2 tablespoons (30 mL) Dijon mustard
2 tablespoons (30 mL) yellow mustard
2 tablespoons (30 mL) Sriracha sauce
1 tablespoon (15 mL) Worcestershire sauce
1 tablespoon (15 mL) vegetable oil
2 teaspoons (10 mL) kosher salt
1 teaspoon (5 mL) cracked black pepper

Creamy Cucumber Old Bay Dip

Makes about 1 cup (250 mL)

½ English cucumber, seeded and coarsely grated
⅔ cup (150 mL) mayonnaise
⅓ cup (75 mL) sour cream
1 tablespoon (15 mL) lemon juice
½ cup (125 mL) finely chopped mixed herbs, such as dill, basil and parsley
1 teaspoon (5 mL) My Old Bay Seasoning (see page 287) or store-bought
Kosher salt and cracked black pepper

To Serve

Sliced English cucumber

A "fizz" is a mixed drink variation on the classic sours family of cocktail. Its defining features are an acidic juice such as lemon or lime and carbonated water. Granted, the cucumber-mint combo is something I am sure you have had before but then you throw basil and elderflower liqueur into the mix and I promise you, this will soon to be your new favourite summer drink.

CUCUMBER GIN FIZZ

Serves 1

4 teaspoons (22 mL) lemon juice
3 slices cucumber
6 mint leaves
4 basil leaves
2 ounces (60 mL) gin
1½ ounces (45 mL) St. Germain
    elderflower liqueur
¼ cup (60 mL) club soda
Thinly sliced cucumber coins or
    ribbons and mint, for garnish

1. Combine lemon juice, cucumber, mint and basil in a cocktail shaker and muddle. Add gin and elderflower liqueur. Fill shaker with ice and shake well.

2. Garnish a highball glass with a cucumber coin and fill with ice. Strain cocktail into glass and top up with club soda. Garnish with cucumber and mint.

EGGPLANT

Most of the summer's bounty is light, bright and juicy. Eggplant is the mysterious smoky-eyed stranger of the bunch. It comes in a wide array of shapes, sizes and colours, from dark purple to pale mauve, from yellow to white. This delicious vegetable has a very neutral taste, with an incredible sponge-like quality. They absorb flavours well and are especially delicious when prepared with lots of garlic, spices and herbs. Charring, grilling and high heat are the keys to bringing out the best quality in eggplant—its almost silky, rich texture. They can be roasted whole and transformed into my Grilled Eggplant and Onion Dip with Sumac Grilled Pita or popped on the grill for my Grilled Eggplant with Mascarpone Cream and Spicy Lemon Honey Vinaigrette—grilling adds a smoky note to its sweet flavour.

When you cook eggplant in its skin, the skin acts as a protective fireproof jacket, and the flesh becomes soft, silky and smoky—the perfect foundation for this dip. The sumac on the pita (a very underrated spice, in my opinion!) brings a wonderfully citrusy note to the dish.

GRILLED EGGPLANT and ONION DIP with SUMAC GRILLED PITA

Make the Grilled Eggplant and Onion Dip

1. Preheat grill to medium-high heat.

2. Grill whole eggplant and onion halves until eggplant softens and onions are slightly charred, about 20 minutes, turning frequently.

3. When cool enough to handle, slice eggplant lengthwise and scoop out 2 cups (500 mL) flesh.

4. In a food processor, combine eggplant flesh, onions, chickpeas, chili, garlic, lemon zest and juice, salt, paprika, cumin, oil and sour cream. Process until smooth. Add water, if necessary, to achieve desired consistency.

Prepare the Sumac Grilled Pitas

5. Whisk together oil, thyme, sumac, salt and pepper. Brush mixture over both sides of pitas and grill over medium heat until golden, about 2 minutes per side.

6. Tear Sumac Grilled Pitas into large pieces and serve immediately with Grilled Eggplant and Onion Dip.

Serves 6

Grilled Eggplant and Onion Dip

1 large Italian eggplant
1 small red onion, halved through the root end
1 cup (250 mL) drained and rinsed canned chickpeas
1 teaspoon (5 mL) minced serrano chili, or more to taste
1 clove garlic, minced, or more to taste
Grated zest and juice of ½ lemon
2 teaspoons (10 mL) kosher salt
2 teaspoons (10 mL) sweet smoked paprika
1 teaspoon (5 mL) ground cumin
⅓ cup (75 mL) extra-virgin olive oil
¼ cup (60 mL) sour cream
1 to 2 tablespoons (15 to 30 mL) water

Sumac Grilled Pitas

¼ cup (60 mL) canola oil
2 tablespoons (30 mL) finely chopped thyme
1 teaspoon (5 mL) sumac
1 teaspoon (5 mL) kosher salt
1 teaspoon (5 mL) cracked black pepper
6 small pita breads

This is a great side dish for those barbecue dinners in the middle of the summer. It's so easy to prepare—it's the first or last item to be put on the barbecue. I love how the creamy mascarpone balances the smokiness from the grill, and then it's all finished off with a little extra sweetness and heat from the Spicy Lemon Honey Vinaigrette. How yummy does that sound!

GRILLED EGGPLANT with MASCARPONE CREAM and SPICY LEMON HONEY VINAIGRETTE

Serves 4 to 6

Spicy Lemon Honey Vinaigrette
Grated zest and juice of ½ lemon
¼ cup (60 mL) honey
2 tablespoons (30 mL) extra-virgin olive oil
1 tablespoon (15 mL) chopped thyme
1 teaspoon (5 mL) minced serrano chili
Kosher salt and cracked black pepper

Mascarpone Cream
½ cup (125 mL) mascarpone cheese
¼ cup (60 mL) whole milk
¼ teaspoon (1 mL) kosher salt
⅛ teaspoon (0.5 mL) cracked black pepper

Spicy Panko Crumbs
2 tablespoons (30 mL) extra-virgin olive oil
½ cup (125 mL) panko bread crumbs
1 teaspoon (5 mL) minced serrano chili
1 teaspoon (5 mL) minced garlic
½ cup (125 mL) finely grated Parmesan cheese

Grilled Eggplant
¼ cup (60 mL) extra-virgin olive oil
1 large Italian eggplant, sliced into ¼-inch (5 mm) rounds
2 graffiti eggplants, sliced into ¼-inch (5 mm) rounds
Kosher salt and cracked black pepper

To Finish
Small basil leaves

Make the Spicy Lemon Honey Vinaigrette
1. In a small bowl, whisk together lemon zest and juice, honey, oil, thyme and chili until combined. Season to taste with salt and pepper.

Make the Mascarpone Cream
2. In a small bowl, whisk together mascarpone, milk, salt and pepper until blended.

Prepare the Spicy Panko Crumbs
3. In a skillet over medium heat, heat oil until shimmering. Add panko, chili and garlic and cook until crumbs are golden brown, about 3 minutes, stirring constantly.

4. Transfer panko mixture to a plate and let cool to room temperature. Add Parmesan and toss to combine.

Grill the Eggplant
5. Preheat grill to medium-high heat. Brush oil over both sides of eggplant slices. Season lightly with salt and pepper and grill until golden brown, turning once, about 2 minutes per side.

6. To serve, fan eggplant slices on a large platter. Drizzle with Spicy Lemon Honey Vinaigrette and Mascarpone Cream. Sprinkle with Spicy Panko Crumbs, garnish with basil leaves and serve immediately.

This harissa paste will become your new favourite rub—it is so full of flavour. The warmth of the cumin, cardamom and coriander blend well with the garlic and the sweetness of the bell peppers. The rub is just as wonderful on chicken, pork and veggies. Make the caponata the day before, to allow the flavours to meld. You could even double the recipe because it will go fast, it's that delicious. If you happen to have any leftovers of this vibrant Sicilian side dish (unlikely!), I love it with pasta and chicken.

HARISSA-SPICED LAMB CHOPS with EGGPLANT CAPONATA

Make the Harissa Paste

1. In a food processor, combine red peppers, garlic, oil, Sriracha, cumin, cardamom and coriander. Process until blended. Season to taste with salt and pepper. Keep refrigerated for up to 2 months.

Marinate the Lamb Chops

2. Place lamb chops in a single layer on a parchment-lined baking sheet and coat both sides of chops with ¼ cup (60 mL) Harissa Paste. Cover and refrigerate for at least 1 hour or overnight. Bring lamb chops to room temperature before grilling.

Make the Eggplant Caponata

3. While lamb chops are marinating, in a large skillet over medium heat, add oil and shallots and cook for 2 minutes. Add garlic and cook for 1 minute more.

4. Stir in celery, eggplant and thyme and cook until eggplant is tender, about 10 minute, stirring occasionally. Add olives, raisins, vinegar, capers and brown sugar and cook for 2 to 3 minutes. Add tomatoes and tomato juice and cook until sauce thickens, about 10 minutes more, stirring occasionally.

5. Remove and discard thyme sprigs. Season caponata to taste with salt and pepper. Keep warm.

Grill the Lamb Chops

6. Preheat grill to medium-high heat. Grill lamb chops until medium-rare, about 4 minutes per side.

7. To serve, spoon Eggplant Caponata onto a warm platter. Arrange chops on top and garnish with mint and parsley.

Serves 4

8 frenched lamb rib chops (3 to 4 ounces/85 to 115 g each)

Harissa Paste
Makes about ¾ cup (175 mL)

3 red bell peppers, seeded and diced
1 tablespoon (15 mL) minced garlic
3 tablespoons (45 mL) extra-virgin olive oil
4 teaspoons (20 mL) Sriracha sauce
2 teaspoons (10 mL) ground cumin
1 teaspoon (5 mL) ground cardamom
1 teaspoon (5 mL) ground coriander
Kosher salt and cracked black pepper

Eggplant Caponata
¼ cup (60 mL) canola oil
2 shallots, diced
2 cloves garlic, chopped
2 ribs celery, cut crosswise into ¼-inch (5 mm) slices
2 cups (500 mL) cubed graffiti eggplant
2 sprigs thyme
¼ cup (60 mL) chopped pitted Kalamata olives
¼ cup (60 mL) seedless sultana raisins
3 tablespoons (45 mL) sherry vinegar
2 tablespoons (30 mL) chopped capers
1 tablespoon (15 mL) dark brown sugar
1½ cups (375 mL) halved tri-colour cherry tomatoes
1 cup (250 mL) tomato juice
Kosher salt and cracked black pepper

To Serve
Mint leaves
Flat-leaf parsley leaves

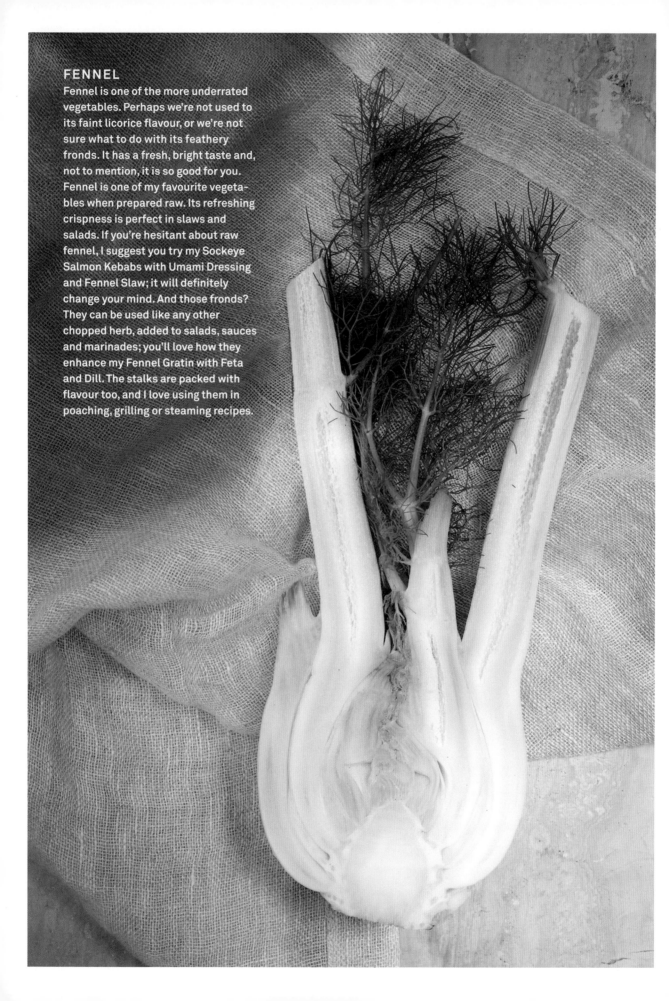

FENNEL

Fennel is one of the more underrated vegetables. Perhaps we're not used to its faint licorice flavour, or we're not sure what to do with its feathery fronds. It has a fresh, bright taste and, not to mention, it is so good for you. Fennel is one of my favourite vegetables when prepared raw. Its refreshing crispness is perfect in slaws and salads. If you're hesitant about raw fennel, I suggest you try my Sockeye Salmon Kebabs with Umami Dressing and Fennel Slaw; it will definitely change your mind. And those fronds? They can be used like any other chopped herb, added to salads, sauces and marinades; you'll love how they enhance my Fennel Gratin with Feta and Dill. The stalks are packed with flavour too, and I love using them in poaching, grilling or steaming recipes.

This recipe will take your grilled chicken game to the next level. By using both olives and their brine in the chicken marinade, you are actually brining the chicken, which helps it stay moist when cooking. I love the Mediterranean flavours of this dish, and I hope it helps transport you there, even just for a moment! Mixing up My Old Bay Seasoning takes no time at all. You can use it to season any number of seafood and chicken dishes.

GRILLED OLIVE FENNEL CHICKEN

Make My Old Bay Seasoning

1. Combine celery salt, celery seeds, mustard, pepper, sweet and smoked paprikas, cloves, ginger, cayenne pepper, mace, cardamom and allspice in a small bowl and mix thoroughly. You can store this in an airtight container in a cool place.

Prepare the Olive Fennel Chicken

2. In a food processor, combine olives, olive brine, garlic, oil, oregano, My Old Bay Seasoning, fennel seeds and chili. Process until blended.

3. In a large bowl, coat chicken pieces with marinade. Cover and refrigerate for at least 30 minutes or overnight.

4. Prepare the grill for indirect cooking over medium heat.

5. Remove chicken from marinade, letting the herbs cling to the chicken. Discard marinade. Grill chicken over indirect heat, with the lid closed as much as possible, until the juices run clear and the internal temperature reaches 160 to 165°F (70 to 74°C) in the thickest part of the thigh (not touching the bone), 45 to 50 minutes, turning once. If desired, to crisp the skin, grill chicken over direct medium heat during the last 5 minutes of grilling time, turning once. Remove chicken from the grill and cover loosely with foil to keep warm while you grill the vegetables.

Serves 4

My Old Bay Seasoning
Makes ½ cup (125 mL)

2 tablespoons (30 mL) celery salt
2 teaspoons (10 mL) ground celery seeds
2 teaspoons (10 mL) dry mustard
2 teaspoons (10 mL) ground black pepper
2 teaspoons (10 mL) sweet paprika
2 teaspoons (10 mL) smoked paprika
1 teaspoon (5 mL) ground cloves
1 teaspoon (5 mL) ground ginger
½ teaspoon (2 mL) cayenne pepper
½ teaspoon (2 mL) mace
½ teaspoon (2 mL) ground cardamom
½ teaspoon (2 mL) ground allspice

Olive Fennel Chicken

1 cup (250 mL) sliced manzanilla olives
⅓ cup (75 mL) brine from jar of manzanilla olives
2 cloves garlic, crushed
¼ cup (60 mL) extra-virgin olive oil
3 tablespoons (45 mL) fresh oregano leaves
1 tablespoon (15 mL) My Old Bay Seasoning
2 teaspoons (10 mL) toasted fennel seeds
1 teaspoon (5 mL) minced serrano chili
1 chicken (about 3 pounds/1.35 kg), backbone removed, chicken cut into 8 pieces

(Recipe continues)

Grilled Summer Vegetables

1 bunch (1 pound/450 g) asparagus, trimmed

8 green onions, trimmed

2 yellow squashes (about 12 ounces/ 340 g total), sliced lengthwise ½ inch (1 cm) thick

2 zucchini (about 12 ounces/340 g total), sliced lengthwise ½ inch (1 cm) thick

2 Japanese eggplants (12 ounces/ 340 g total), sliced lengthwise ½ inch (1 cm) thick

2 small fennel bulbs, stalks trimmed, fronds removed and quartered

1 red bell pepper, seeded and halved

¼ cup (60 mL) plus 2 tablespoons (30 mL) olive oil

Kosher salt and cracked black pepper

3 tablespoons (45 mL) balsamic vinegar

2 cloves garlic, minced

1 teaspoon (5 mL) chopped flat-leaf parsley

1 teaspoon (5 mL) chopped basil

½ teaspoon (2 mL) finely chopped rosemary

To Serve

Mixed whole olives

Oregano sprigs

Grill the Summer Vegetables

6. Increase the barbecue heat to medium-high. While chicken rests, brush vegetables with ¼ cup (60 mL) oil to coat lightly and season with salt and pepper. Working in batches, grill vegetables until tender and lightly charred all over: 4 minutes for the asparagus and green onions; 7 minutes for the yellow squash, zucchini, eggplant and fennel; 8 to 10 minutes for the bell peppers. (The key to getting those great grill marks is to not shift the vegetables too frequently once they've been placed on the hot grill.) Arrange vegetables on a platter.

7. Whisk remaining 2 tablespoons (30 mL) oil, balsamic vinegar, garlic, parsley, basil and rosemary in a small bowl to blend. Season to taste with salt and pepper. Drizzle herb mixture over vegetables.

8. Serve vegetables warm with Olive Fennel Chicken, garnished with mixed whole olives and oregano sprigs.

Umami is one of the five tastes, along with sweetness, sourness, bitterness and saltiness, and is the flavour associated with wonderfully rich and savoury foods. The umami flavour in this delicious dressing will make your taste buds sing. It is almost magical when paired with just-caught sockeye salmon. And even better, it can be made ahead of time.

SOCKEYE SALMON KEBABS with UMAMI DRESSING and FENNEL SLAW

Serves 6

Umami Dressing
Makes 1¼ cups (300 mL)
1 tablespoon (15 mL) canola oil
1-inch (2.5 cm) piece fresh ginger, peeled and thinly sliced
3 cloves garlic, thinly sliced
1 chipotle pepper in adobo sauce, chopped
1 Granny Smith apple, cored and thinly sliced
1 cup (250 mL) coarsely chopped shiitake mushroom stems and caps
½ cup (125 mL) soy sauce
½ cup (125 mL) pineapple juice
¼ cup (60 mL) sherry vinegar
2 tablespoons (30 mL) honey
2 teaspoons (10 mL) fish sauce
4 large egg yolks
1 cup (250 mL) canola oil

Sockeye Salmon Kebabs
3 tablespoons (45 mL) soy sauce
2 tablespoons (30 mL) sesame oil
2 tablespoons (30 mL) canola oil
2 tablespoons (30 mL) honey
2 tablespoons (30 mL) minced peeled fresh ginger
2 tablespoons (30 mL) finely chopped cilantro
1 tablespoon (15 mL) lemon juice
1 serrano chili, seeded and minced
1 side skinless sockeye salmon (about 2 pounds/900 g), trimmed and cut into pieces 2 inches (5 cm) square
12 bamboo skewers, soaked in cold water for 20 minutes

Make the Umami Dressing
1. In a large saucepan, combine oil, ginger, garlic and chipotle pepper. Cook over medium heat for 1 minute. Add apple and mushrooms and continue cooking for 5 minutes. Stir in soy sauce, pineapple juice, sherry vinegar, honey and fish sauce. Simmer for 15 to 20 minutes, until liquid has reduced to ⅓ cup (75 mL). Strain liquid (discarding the solids) and cool to room temperature.

2. Pour cooled liquid into a food processor; add egg yolks. With the processor running, slowly add oil in a steady stream. The dressing should have the consistency of mayonnaise. Dressing can be refrigerated in an airtight container for up to 2 weeks

Marinate the Salmon
3. In a large bowl, whisk together soy sauce, sesame and canola oils, honey, ginger, cilantro, lemon juice and chili until combined. Gently fold in salmon pieces. Cover and refrigerate for 1 hour to allow flavours to meld.

Make the Fennel Slaw

4. While salmon is marinating, in a large bowl, whisk lemon juice, honey, shallots, mustard and olive oil until well blended. Add celery, celery leaves, fennel, fennel fronds, apple and mint; toss to coat. Season to taste with salt and pepper.

Grill the Salmon Kebabs

5. Prepare the grill for indirect cooking over high heat. Thread 3 marinated salmon pieces onto 2 skewers so the salmon is well secured. Repeat with remaining salmon and skewers; reserve remaining marinade.

6. Grill kebabs over indirect high heat, with the lid closed, until opaque throughout, 4 to 5 minutes. During the last 2 minutes of grilling time, brush kebabs with reserved marinade. Transfer kebabs to serving plates and serve warm with Umami Dressing and Fennel Slaw.

Fennel Slaw

3 tablespoons (45 mL) lemon juice

2 tablespoons (30 mL) honey

1 tablespoon (15 mL) minced shallot or red onion

½ teaspoon (2 mL) whole-grain mustard

¼ cup (60 mL) olive oil

2 ribs celery, thinly sliced on the diagonal

¼ cup (60 mL) loosely packed celery leaves

2 small fennel bulbs, trimmed, cored and thinly sliced crosswise

¼ cup (60 mL) chopped fennel fronds

1 apple, such as Gala or Granny Smith, julienned

2 tablespoons (30 mL) coarsely chopped mint

Kosher salt and cracked black pepper

Looking for a new side dish? Reinvent a classic gratin by using fennel. This summer vegetable is such a versatile ingredient with its slight anise flavour, and it's a perfect partner for sweet onions, salty feta and fresh dill. This dish is at home beside any fish or roast chicken—and a good glass of Viognier!

FENNEL GRATIN with FETA and DILL

1. Preheat oven to 375°F (190°C) and grease a 4-cup (1 L) baking dish.

2. In a large skillet over medium heat, heat oil. Add fennel and onions and cook until vegetables have softened, about 15 minutes, stirring often.

3. Add garlic and cook for 1 minute more, then stir in dill. Remove from heat and let mixture cool slightly.

4. In a large bowl, beat eggs, then stir in feta. Fold in cooled fennel mixture and season to taste with salt and pepper. Spoon mixture into baking dish and sprinkle with fennel fronds.

5. Bake until set in the centre and golden at the sides, about 35 minutes. Transfer to a wire rack and let cool for 10 minutes before serving.

Serves 6

2 tablespoons (30 mL) olive oil
2 pounds (900 g) fennel, trimmed, quartered, cored and thinly sliced crosswise (about 4 cups/1 L)
2 yellow onions, thinly sliced
2 large cloves garlic, minced
½ cup (125 mL) chopped dill
3 large eggs
4 ounces (115 g) feta cheese, crumbled
Kosher salt and cracked black pepper
¼ cup (60 mL) chopped fennel fronds

MELONS

It's not officially summer until you cut into a melon. Bring on the honeydews, cantaloupes and watermelons. It is delicious served on its own, piled high on your summer picnic table. But it's also terrific blended with tequila—can you think of anything more summery than a Watermelon Margarita? And it's just as scrumptious on top of grilled fish or tacos, like in my Jerk Shrimp Tostadas with Minted Melon Salsa. It doesn't matter how you slice it, melon is the coolest, most refreshing fruit.

This margarita doesn't need much sugar because of the natural sweetness the watermelon offers. A little bit of fresh lime juice brightens the drink and adds a welcome tanginess. A truly refreshing cocktail for those hot summer days.

WATERMELON MARGARITA

1. In a mini food processor, combine salt, mint leaves and lime zest and process until mixture turns green and resembles wet sand. Scrape mixture into a shallow bowl.

2. Moisten rim of a cocktail glass with lime wedge, set in salt mixture and twist to coat. Set aside.

3. Muddle watermelon and sugar until pulpy and mostly juice. Strain through a fine-mesh sieve, pressing down on watermelon to extract as much juice as possible. Pour into prepared glass. Add tequila, triple sec and lime juice, and stir to mix everything together. Add desired amount of ice, garnish glass with a watermelon wedge and serve.

Serves 1

¼ cup (60 mL) kosher salt

4 sprigs mint, leaves only

Grated zest of 1 lime

Lime wedge, to rim glass

1 cup (250 mL) chopped watermelon

2 teaspoons (10 mL) granulated sugar, or to taste

1½ ounces (45 mL) tequila

1 ounce (30 mL) triple sec or other citrus-flavoured liquor

1 tablespoon (15 mL) freshly squeezed lime juice

Small watermelon wedge, for garnish

Summer salads are all about the combination of sweet fruit and bitter greens to balance out the plate. So in this recipe I combine sweet melon with chili and aromatic basil and mint, and finish it off with a little bitter radicchio. There are so many wonderful flavours at play here, and the feta cream is a delicious addition. The feta is combined with sour cream to create a silky dressing that still honours the feta's brininess.

MELON SALAD with FETA CREAM and CHILI HONEY VINAIGRETTE

Make the Feta Cream
1. Stir together sour cream and feta until combined. Season to taste with salt and pepper. Cover and refrigerate until ready to serve.

Make the Chili Honey Vinaigrette
2. In a small bowl, whisk together oil, lemon zest, lemon juice, honey and chili until blended. Season to taste with salt and pepper.

Assemble the Melon Salad
3. Spoon Feta Cream onto each chilled salad plate. Divide cantaloupe, cucumber, radicchio, mint leaves and basil leaves on top. Drizzle with Chili Honey Vinaigrette and serve immediately.

Serves 4

Feta Cream
½ cup (125 mL) sour cream
½ cup (125 mL) crumbled feta cheese
Kosher salt and cracked black pepper

Chili Honey Vinaigrette
2 tablespoons (30 mL) extra-virgin
 olive oil
½ teaspoon (2 mL) grated lemon zest
1 tablespoon (15 mL) lemon juice
1 teaspoon (5 mL) honey
1 teaspoon (5 mL) minced Fresno chili
Kosher salt and cracked black pepper

For Assembly
½ cantaloupe, peeled, seeded and cut
 into 1-inch (2.5 cm) cubes
2 mini cucumbers, halved lengthwise
 and sliced into thin wedges
1 head radicchio, torn
¼ cup (60 mL) mint leaves, for garnish
¼ cup (60 mL) basil leaves, for garnish

Everyone loves a little jerk, whether it's on chicken or shrimp. I worked on this recipe after I came back from cooking at an event in Jamaica, so I can guarantee it's the real deal. There are lots of ingredients, but it's not as complicated as it might look. The jerk seasoning is easily adaptable, so you can tweak this base recipe to make it your own. If you like more heat, add more chilies!

JERK SHRIMP TOSTADAS with MINTED MELON SALSA

Serves 4

1 pound (450 g) large shrimp (size 21–25), peeled and deveined

Jerk Seasoning
1 bunch green onions, trimmed and coarsely chopped
1 or 2 Scotch bonnet peppers
2 tablespoons (30 mL) chopped thyme
2 teaspoons (10 mL) ground allspice
2 teaspoons (10 mL) cinnamon
1 teaspoon (5 mL) nutmeg
1 tablespoon (15 mL) dark brown sugar
2 teaspoons (10 mL) kosher salt
2 teaspoons (10 mL) black pepper
¼ cup (60 mL) white vinegar
2 tablespoons (30 mL) olive oil, plus extra for brushing shrimp

Minted Melon Salsa
2 cups (500 mL) diced honeydew melon
1 teaspoon (5 mL) finely chopped mint
1 teaspoon (5 mL) minced jalapeño pepper
2 tablespoons (30 mL) lime juice
1 tablespoon (15 mL) honey

To Serve
4 crispy corn tostadas
1 cup (250 mL) shredded Little Gem lettuce
Cilantro leaves
Lime wedges
Chipotle Aïoli (see page 128)

Make the Jerk Seasoning
1. In a blender, combine green onions, peppers, thyme, allspice, cinnamon, nutmeg, brown sugar, salt, black pepper, vinegar and oil. Process until blended. This seasoning can be refrigerated in an airtight container for up to 5 days.

Make the Minted Melon Salsa
2. In a medium bowl, gently toss together melon, mint, jalapeño, lime juice and honey until combined. Cover and refrigerate until ready to serve.

Prepare the Shrimp
3. Place shrimp in a bowl and toss with ½ cup (125 mL) Jerk Seasoning until fully coated. Allow to marinate for 30 minutes at room temperature.

4. Preheat and prepare the grill for direct cooking over medium heat.

5. Lightly brush the shrimp with oil and then season them with more of the Jerk Seasoning. Brush the cooking grates clean. Grill the shrimp over direct high heat, with the lid closed as much as possible, until slightly firm on the surface and opaque in the centre, 2 to 4 minutes, turning once. Remove from the grill and set aside.

Assemble the Tostadas
6. Place a tostada on each plate, top with lettuce, shrimp and Minted Melon Salsa. Serve immediately garnished with cilantro leaves, lime wedges and a dollop of chipotle aïoli.

STONE FRUITS

When stone fruit season is in full swing,
I have a hard time resisting all those
colours, textures and aromas. Stone fruits
are perfect in shortcakes and tarts; their
light, juicy sweetness deepens into a
wonderful jamminess as they cook. I love
adding them to salsas and salads as well;
my Apricot Arugula Salad with Prosciutto
and Burrata is absolutely delicious.
They're also a great addition to vinaigrettes, marinades and sauces—peaches
add a delectable sweetness to my
Bourbon-Peach Barbecued Ribs with
Broccoli Slaw. Or you can have a little fun
and whip up a cocktail—stone fruits pair
really well with bourbon. I suggest my
cooling Apricot Bourbon Sour for a hot
summer evening.

This is my twist on classic barbecue ribs and slaw. I love using perfectly ripe peaches in my barbecue sauce in the summer, when they are at their peak, so juicy and full of flavour. Using broccoli instead of cabbage brings a cool, crunchy and savoury element to the slaw. To save on time, make the barbecue sauce up to 2 weeks ahead.

BOURBON-PEACH BARBECUED RIBS with BROCCOLI SLAW

Make the Bourbon-Peach Barbecue Sauce

1. In a large saucepan over medium-high heat, melt butter. Add onions and cook until translucent, stirring often. Season with salt and pepper. Stir in garlic and diced peaches. Continue to cook for another 2 to 3 minutes. Lower the heat and add chipotle peppers, peach nectar, tomatoes, tomato paste, vinegar, bourbon, brown sugar, mustard, molasses, chili powder and paprika. Stir well and bring to a boil. Lower the heat and simmer, uncovered, for 1 hour to allow the sauce to thicken and reduce.

2. Pour sauce into a food processor or blender and process until smooth. Transfer to an airtight container and allow to cool. Keep refrigerated for up to 2 weeks.

Make the Broccoli Slaw

3. In a large bowl, toss together broccoli florets and shaved stalks, carrots, jalapeño, peanuts and mint.

4. In a small bowl, whisk together vinegar and mustard. Whisk in oil a few drops at a time until emulsified, then season with salt and pepper. Toss broccoli mixture with dressing. Keep refrigerated until ready to serve.

Serves 4 to 6

6 pounds (2.7 kg) pork baby back ribs

Bourbon-Peach Barbecue Sauce
Makes 4 cups (1 L)
2 tablespoons (30 mL) unsalted butter
1 medium sweet onion, diced
Kosher salt and cracked black pepper
4 cloves garlic, minced
6 large peaches, peeled, pitted and diced
3 chipotle peppers in adobo sauce, coarsely chopped
1¼ cups (300 mL) peach nectar
1 can (14 ounces/398 mL) diced tomatoes
¾ cup (175 mL) tomato paste
½ cup (125 mL) apple cider vinegar
¾ cup (175 mL) bourbon
¾ cup (175 mL) dark brown sugar
3 tablespoons (45 mL) Dijon mustard
2 tablespoons (30 mL) molasses
1 teaspoon (5 mL) chili powder
1 teaspoon (5 mL) smoked paprika

Broccoli Slaw
2 cups (500 mL) broccoli florets
½ cup (125 mL) peeled and shaved broccoli stalks
½ cup (125 mL) julienned carrots
1 jalapeño pepper, grilled, peeled, seeded and minced
½ cup (125 mL) coarsely chopped roasted peanuts
6 mint leaves, coarsely chopped
¼ cup (60 mL) sherry vinegar
1 tablespoon (15 mL) whole-grain mustard (I like Kozlik's Sweet and Smokey Mustard)
½ cup (125 mL) canola oil
Kosher salt and cracked black pepper

(Recipe continues)

Dry Rub

3 tablespoons (45 mL) dark brown
    sugar
1 tablespoon (15 mL) chili powder
1 tablespoon (15 mL) salt
2 teaspoons (10 mL) cracked black
    pepper
1 teaspoon (5 mL) dry mustard
½ teaspoon (2 mL) garlic powder
½ teaspoon (2 mL) onion powder

Grilled Peaches

2 tablespoons (30 mL) unsalted butter
1 tablespoon (15 mL) granulated
    sugar
4 medium peaches, firm but ripe,
    halved and pitted

Make the Dry Rub and Prepare the Ribs

5. In a bowl, combine brown sugar, chili powder, salt, black pepper, mustard, garlic powder and onion powder. Place ribs on a baking sheet and rub both sides with spice rub. Cover and refrigerate for at least 2 hours or overnight.

Barbecue the Ribs

6. Prepare the grill for direct cooking over medium heat.

7. Using eight 18- × 24-inch (46 × 60 cm) sheets of heavy-duty foil, double-wrap each rack in its own packet. Place ribs on the grill over direct heat, close the lid and cook for 1 hour, occasionally turning the packets over for even cooking, making sure not to pierce the foil. Remove packets from the grill and let rest for about 10 minutes. Carefully remove the ribs and discard rendered fat and foil.

8. Grill ribs over direct heat, with the lid closed as much as possible, until they are sizzling and lightly charred, 10 to 12 minutes, turning and basting once or twice with the Bourbon-Peach Barbecue Sauce. Remove from the grill and tent loosely with foil to keep warm.

Make the Grilled Peaches

9. In a small saucepan over medium heat, melt the butter. Add the sugar and stir to dissolve. Remove the saucepan from the heat. Brush the peach halves all over with the butter mixture.

10. Brush the barbecue's cooking grates clean again. Grill the peach halves over direct medium heat, with the lid closed as much as possible, until they are browned in spots and warm throughout, 8 to 10 minutes, turning every 3 minutes or so. Remove the peaches from the grill and set aside.

11. Cut racks into individual ribs and serve with Broccoli Slaw, peaches and additional Bourbon-Peach Barbecue Sauce.

This salad should be made when apricots are in season, but if you missed that short window, it's just as wonderful with any ripe stone fruit. I love serving this crowd-pleaser at an al fresco dinner or picnic. Don't be shy with the prosciutto and burrata—they are the stars here.

APRICOT ARUGULA SALAD with PROSCIUTTO and BURRATA

1. Arrange arugula on a serving platter. Top with radishes, prosciutto, apricots and burrata.

2. In a small bowl, whisk together vinegar, lime zest, lime juice, green onions and chili, then slowly whisk in oil until emulsified.

3. Spoon vinaigrette over salad, then top with pine nuts and mint. Season to taste with salt and pepper.

Serves 4

4 cups (1 L) packed arugula

4 radishes, sliced into thin rounds

8 slices prosciutto

2 to 4 large apricots, pitted and sliced into wedges

1 cup (250 mL) burrata cheese torn into small pieces

2 tablespoons (30 mL) sherry vinegar

1 teaspoon (5 mL) grated lime zest

2 tablespoons (30 mL) lime juice

2 green onions, green part only, thinly sliced on the diagonal

½ teaspoon (2 mL) minced serrano chili

¼ cup (60 mL) olive oil

¼ cup (60 mL) toasted pine nuts

8 small mint leaves

Kosher salt and cracked black pepper

Duck is often paired with something sweet, so here I've crusted it with a mixture of five-spice, finely chopped walnuts and brown sugar. The sugar burns slightly as the meat roasts, forming a bittersweet crust that pairs beautifully with the juicy richness of the duck. And I love this plum chutney—its sweetness is the perfect accompaniment to duck, but it's also delicious on toast!

WALNUT and FIVE-SPICE CRUSTED DUCK BREAST with PLUM CHUTNEY

Serves 6

Plum Chutney

1 tablespoon (15 mL) unsalted butter
2 teaspoons (10 mL) dark brown sugar
½ teaspoon (2 mL) minced peeled fresh ginger
⅛ teaspoon (0.5 mL) cinnamon
⅛ teaspoon (0.5 mL) ground cloves
Pinch of red pepper flakes
2 cups (500 mL) thin plum wedges
2 tablespoons (30 mL) seasoned rice vinegar

Walnut and Five-Spice Rub

½ cup (125 mL) finely chopped walnuts
2 teaspoons (10 mL) five-spice powder
1 teaspoon (5 mL) dark brown sugar
1 teaspoon (5 mL) kosher salt
¼ teaspoon (1 mL) cracked black pepper

Duck Breasts

2 large duck breasts (about 1 pound/450 g each)
Kosher salt and cracked black pepper

Make the Plum Chutney

1. In a medium skillet over medium heat, melt butter. Add sugar, ginger, cinnamon, cloves and red pepper flakes and cook until sugar dissolves and begins to caramelize, about 1 minute, stirring frequently.

2. Add plums and cook until they begin to soften, about 5 minutes, tossing occasionally. Pour in vinegar and cook for 2 minutes more, stirring frequently. Remove from heat. If not using immediately, chutney can be stored in the refrigerator for up to 2 weeks.

Make the Walnut and Five-Spice Rub

3. Stir together walnuts, five-spice powder, sugar, salt and pepper until blended.

Make the Duck

4. Preheat oven to 425°F (220°C). Pat duck breasts dry with paper towel. Trim excess fat from around breasts, then make incisions into the skin in a cross-hatch pattern, being careful not to cut into the meat.

5. Heat an ovenproof skillet over medium heat. Season both sides of duck breast with salt and pepper, then place skin side down in skillet and cook for 8 minutes to render the fat. Turn breasts over and cook for 2 minutes more, then transfer to a plate. Drain fat from skillet.

6. Return duck breasts to skillet and coat skin side of each breast with about ¼ cup (60 mL) Walnut and Five-Spice Rub. Transfer to oven and roast until internal temperature reaches 140°F (60°C) for medium-rare doneness.

7. Tent duck breasts with foil and let rest for 10 minutes. Slice on the diagonal into 1-inch (2.5 cm) slices and serve with Plum Chutney.

My favourite drinks generally all have something in common—bourbon—but if I had to choose just one, it would probably be a bourbon sour. This is my version of the classic, using beautiful apricots. This delicious stone fruit is particularly special since they have a such a short season in Canada, so make sure to enjoy them in the summer while they're fresh and juicy! If you miss apricots, don't despair—peaches are equally at home in this cocktail. Make sure to plan ahead, as you'll need to start infusing the bourbon a week ahead of time.

APRICOT BOURBON SOUR

Make the Simple Syrup

1. Combine water and sugar in a small saucepan and heat over medium heat, stirring until sugar dissolves. Let cool before using. Simple syrup will keep in a sealed container in the refrigerator for up to 2 weeks.

Infuse the Apricot Bourbon

2. Place fresh and dried apricots in a clean 1-quart (1 L) mason jar. Pour in bourbon to cover the fruit. Seal the jar and set aside to infuse for 1 week at room temperature.

Finish the Apricot Bourbon

3. After a week, strain bourbon through a fine-mesh sieve, discarding the fruit. In a clean mason jar, combine strained bourbon and Simple Syrup. Stir to combine. Bourbon can be stored in the sealed jar in the refrigerator for up to 2 months.

Prepare the Cocktail

4. To a cocktail shaker filled with ice, add apricot juice and Apricot Bourbon. Shake for 10 seconds. Strain into a cocktail glass, add one or two lemon and lime rounds and ice and serve immediately.

Serves 1

Simple Syrup
1 cup (250 mL) water
1 cup (250 mL) granulated sugar

Apricot Bourbon
Makes enough for 7 drinks
¾ cup (175 mL) pitted and diced fresh apricots
¾ cup (175 mL) diced unsweetened dried apricots
1½ cups (375 mL) bourbon
¼ cup (60 mL) Simple Syrup

Apricot Bourbon Sour
⅔ cup (150 mL) apricot juice
2 ounces (60 mL) Apricot Bourbon
Thinly sliced lemon and lime rounds, for garnish

During the height of summer, grilled or sautéed peaches make this sundae an ideal treat. To ensure your fruit holds its shape when cooking, choose peaches that are ripe but firm. Homemade ice creams and sorbets are the only way to go; they are so simple to make, and you can change the flavours so easily depending on the season and the type of fruit you have on hand. This vanilla ice cream is my go-to recipe and is endlessly customizable.

PEACH MELBA SUNDAE

Make the Vanilla Ice Cream

1. In a medium bowl, whisk egg yolks. In a medium saucepan, combine cream, milk, sugar and vanilla bean and seeds. Place over medium heat and cook, stirring, until beginning to steam, about 5 minutes.

2. Whisking constantly, add ¼ cup (60 mL) hot cream mixture to yolks, then stir yolk mixture into pot of hot cream. Cook over medium heat, stirring constantly with a wooden spoon, until custard is thick enough to coat the back of the spoon, 4 to 5 minutes. Pour custard through a fine-mesh sieve into a bowl and let cool completely. Refrigerate until chilled, at least 2 hours.

3. Pour chilled custard into an ice cream maker and process according to the manufacturer's instructions. Transfer to an airtight container and freeze until set, at least 4 hours and up to 1 week.

Make the Raspberry Sorbet

4. In a food processor, combine raspberries and water. Pulse until mixture is smooth. Press raspberry purée through a fine-mesh sieve over a bowl to remove the seeds, then transfer to a medium bowl. Add sugar and lemon juice and whisk until sugar is dissolved. Process sorbet in an ice cream maker according to manufacturer's instructions. Transfer to an airtight container and freeze until set, at least 4 hours and up to 1 week.

Make the Amaretti Cookies

5. Preheat oven to 325°F (160°C) and line a baking sheet with parchment paper.

6. In a large bowl, beat egg whites until soft peaks form. Add 1 cup (250 mL) sugar, a few tablespoons at a time, unit stiff, glossy peaks form. Beat in almond extract, then fold in ground almonds with a spatula.

7. Spoon generous tablespoons of dough onto the baking sheet, leaving 2 inches (5 cm) between each cookie. Sprinkle with 2 tablespoons (30 mL) sugar. Bake for 18 to 20 minutes, until light brown and firm to the touch. Transfer baking sheet to a wire rack and let amaretti cool to room temperature. Cookies can be stored in a sealed jar at room temperature for up to 4 days.

(Recipe continues)

Serves 4

Vanilla Ice Cream
Makes 4 cups (1 L)
8 large egg yolks (reserve 2 egg whites for Amaretti Cookies)
3 cups (750 mL) heavy (35%) cream
1 cup (250 mL) whole milk
1 cup (250 mL) granulated sugar
1 vanilla bean, split lengthwise and seeds scraped out

Raspberry Sorbet
Makes about 6 cups (1.5 L)
6 cups (1.5 L) raspberries
¾ cup (175 mL) water
1½ cups (375 mL) granulated sugar
2 tablespoons (30 mL) lemon juice
Pinch of kosher salt

Amaretti Cookies
Makes 24 cookies
2 large egg whites
1 cup (250 mL) plus 2 tablespoons (30 mL) granulated sugar, divided
½ teaspoon (2 mL) almond extract
2¼ cups (550 mL) ground almonds

Caramel Sauce

Makes about 1 cup (250 mL)

1 cup (250 mL) granulated sugar
¼ cup (60 mL) water
Pinch of salt
2 tablespoons (30 mL) unsalted butter
2 tablespoons (30 mL) heavy (35%)
   cream

Glazed Peaches

2 cups (500 mL) peeled, pitted and
   sliced peaches
⅓ cup (75 mL) pure maple syrup
1 vanilla bean, split lengthwise

To Serve

1 cup (250 mL) whole raspberries
½ cup (125 mL) crumbled Amaretti
   Cookies
¼ cup (60 mL) sliced toasted almonds

Make the Caramel Sauce

8. Shortly before serving, in a small saucepan, stir together sugar, water and salt. Bring to a boil over medium-high heat and cook, without stirring or shaking the pot, until water has evaporated and sugar is light golden brown, about 8 minutes. Remove from heat and whisk in butter and cream until smooth. Keep sauce warm.

Prepare the Glazed Peaches

9. In a medium saucepan, combine peaches, maple syrup and vanilla bean. Cook over medium heat until peaches are barely tender and syrup thickens, about 15 minutes. Remove from heat and let cool slightly. Discard vanilla bean.

Assemble the Sundaes

10. Spoon 2 scoops each of Vanilla Ice Cream and Raspberry Sorbet into 4 chilled bowls. Sprinkle with raspberries, crumbled Amaretti Cookies and almonds. Drizzle with Caramel Sauce, top with Glazed Peaches and serve immediately.

TOMATOES

The reigning queen of summer has to be the tomato. There are so many lovely heirloom varieties, and no matter which you choose, a tomato really is perfect on its own. A freshly picked tomato's colour, smell and flavour can't be beat, so when I'm serving them, I keep things simple: a touch of salt to bring out their natural sweetness, perhaps a handful of torn fresh basil, and a healthy amount of peppery new olive oil and nuggets of salty Parmesan cheese. Or try my Grilled Summer Tomato Salad with Basil Vinaigrette for another lovely way to serve fresh tomatoes. There is an endless list of incredible tomato recipes for the summer, so when the bushels are plentiful at the market, grab as many as you can and cook up some of these dishes!

There are a few reasons why you may not automatically think of tomatoes when you think of grilling. First, there's all this talk that nothing beats a ripe, just-off-the-vine tomato. But I just can't resist what grilling does to a tomato, intensifying its flavour by concentrating its juices and giving its skin a smoky flavour.

GRILLED SUMMER TOMATO SALAD with BASIL VINAIGRETTE

Serves 4

Basil Vinaigrette
Makes about 1 cup (250 mL)
½ cup (125 mL) fresh basil leaves
¼ cup (60 mL) white wine vinegar
1 tablespoon (15 mL) honey
1 tablespoon (15 mL) lemon juice
½ cup (125 mL) olive oil
Kosher salt and cracked black pepper

Grilled Tomato Salad
2 large vine-ripened tomatoes, cut
    into ½-inch (1 cm) rounds
2 beefsteak tomatoes, cut into ½-inch
    (1 cm) rounds
Kosher salt and cracked black pepper
¼ cup (60 mL) canola oil
¼ cup (60 mL) sherry vinegar
1 clove garlic, minced
½ teaspoon (2 mL) minced red chili
10 tri-coloured cherry tomatoes,
    halved through the stem end
Basil, oregano and thyme leaves,
    for garnish

Make the Basil Vinaigrette
1. In a blender, combine basil, vinegar, honey, lemon juice and oil. Purée until smooth. Season to taste with salt and pepper.

Prepare the Grilled Tomato Salad
2. Prepare the grill for direct cooking over medium heat. Brush the grates clean and wipe with a cloth dipped in oil.

3. Season the vine-ripened and beefsteak tomatoes with salt and pepper. Grill over direct heat, with the lid closed as much as possible, 1 to 2 minutes per side. Transfer the grilled tomatoes to a bowl.

4. Whisk together oil, vinegar, garlic and chili until blended. Pour over grilled tomatoes and let rest for 5 minutes to allow flavours to meld.

5. Plate grilled tomatoes and cherry tomatoes and spoon Basil Vinaigrette over top. Garnish with fresh basil, oregano and thyme leaves.

When you think tomatoes, you think basil, but when you think cucumbers, you reach for dill. In this tomato and cucumber salad, I've used dill instead of basil, and you'll be surprised how well it works. Soon you will use fresh dill in everything!

TOMATO CUCUMBER SALAD with FETA and DILL VINAIGRETTE

Serves 4

1. In a small saucepan over medium heat, cook onions, sugar and vinegar until sugar dissolves and onions soften, about 10 minutes. With a slotted spoon, transfer onions to a plate to cool. Reserve 3 tablespoons (45 mL) pickling liquid in a small bowl.

2. Preheat grill to medium. Cut baguette into ½-inch (1 cm) slices and brush both sides with ¼ cup (60 mL) olive oil. Grill until toasted. Tear into bite-sized pieces and place croutons in a large bowl. Add cherry tomatoes, tomato wedges, cucumber, capers and reserved pickled onions.

3. To the reserved pickling liquid, add pickled jalapeño, mustard and dill, then whisk in the remaining ½ cup (125 mL) olive oil, a few drops at a time, until combined. Season to taste with salt and pepper. Spoon over tomato-bread mixture and toss gently to combine.

4. Arrange mixed greens on a serving platter. Spoon tomato-bread mixture over greens, sprinkle with feta and garnish with dill sprigs.

½ cup (125 mL) thinly sliced red onions
¼ cup (60 mL) granulated sugar
¼ cup (60 mL) sherry vinegar
½ baguette
¾ cup (175 mL) extra-virgin olive oil, divided
1 pint (500 mL) tri-coloured cherry tomatoes, quartered
1 each small yellow, red and orange tomatoes, cored and sliced into 8 wedges
1 small English cucumber, halved lengthwise and cut diagonally into ¼-inch (5 mm) slices
1 tablespoon (15 mL) chopped capers
2 tablespoons (30 mL) minced pickled jalapeño peppers
1 tablespoon (15 mL) Dijon mustard
1 teaspoon (5 mL) finely chopped dill
Kosher salt and cracked black pepper
4 cups (1 L) mixed greens
¾ cup (175 mL) crumbled feta cheese
Dill sprigs, for garnish

Halibut is my hands-down favourite white fish. It's a lean fish, with mild, sweet-tasting flesh and a firm but tender texture. It is delicious served with ripe, juicy tomatoes and is the perfect partner for the sweet Dungeness crab and creamy jalapeño dressing in this dish.

HALIBUT with HEIRLOOM TOMATOES, SPINACH and CREAMY JALAPEÑO DUNGENESS CRAB

Serves 4

Halibut
Grated zest and juice of 1 lemon
2 cloves garlic, crushed
4 to 6 basil leaves, thinly sliced
2 teaspoons (10 mL) capers, finely chopped
¼ cup (60 mL) olive oil, divided
4 skinless halibut fillets (5 to 6 ounces/140 to 170 g each)
Kosher salt and cracked black pepper

Crab Salad
¼ cup (60 mL) sour cream
¼ cup (60 mL) mayonnaise
1 jalapeño pepper, grilled, seeded and finely chopped
1 teaspoon (5 mL) lemon zest
1 tablespoon (15 mL) lemon juice
1 tablespoon (15 mL) finely chopped chives
Kosher salt and cracked black pepper
½ pound (225 g) steamed Dungeness crabmeat, picked over

To Serve
1 pound (450 g) large ripe heirloom tomatoes, cut into ½-inch (1 cm) rounds
2 cups (500 mL) baby spinach
1 tablespoon (15 mL) finely diced shallot
3 tablespoons (45 mL) balsamic vinegar
¼ cup (60 mL) extra-virgin olive oil
Kosher salt and cracked black pepper

Prepare the Halibut
1. In a small bowl, whisk together lemon zest and juice, garlic, basil, capers and 2 tablespoons (30 mL) olive oil. Pour over halibut and marinate in the refrigerator for at least 2 hours. Bring to room temperature before cooking.

Make the Crab Salad
2. In a small bowl, whisk together sour cream, mayonnaise, jalapeño, lemon zest, lemon juice and chives. Season to taste with salt and pepper. Place crab in a large bowl and, using a spatula, gently fold in dressing 1 tablespoon (15 mL) at a time. Season to taste with salt and pepper. Keep refrigerated until ready to serve.

Cook the Halibut
3. Season halibut with salt and pepper. Heat a large skillet over medium-high heat. Add remaining 2 tablespoons (30 mL) olive oil and carefully lay the fish in the pan. Cook for 3 to 4 minutes, until browned. Turn fish over, lower the heat to medium-low, and cook for a few more minutes, until just cooked through, flaky and opaque in the centre.

4. To serve, arrange sliced tomatoes and spinach on dinner plates. In a small bowl, whisk together shallots, balsamic vinegar and extra-virgin olive oil; season with salt and pepper. Spoon vinaigrette over tomatoes and spinach. Place halibut on top of tomato salad, then spoon Crab Salad on top of the halibut. Serve immediately.

When it comes to cooking steak dishes in the summer, I want something fresh and bright to serve alongside. So why not charred tomatoes, topped with the saltiness and bite of a blue cheese. If blue cheese isn't for you, feta or goat cheese also work nicely.

GRILLED FLANK STEAK with CHARRED BEEFSTEAK TOMATOES and BLUE CHEESE

Make the Marinade and Prepare the Flank Steak

1. In a food processor, combine oil, thyme, parsley, cilantro, mustard, salt and pepper. Process until smooth. Slather mixture over both sides of steak, cover and let marinate in refrigerator for 1 hour.

2. Prepare the grill for direct cooking over high heat.

3. Grill the steak over direct heat, with the lid closed, until cooked to your desired doneness, 6 to 8 minutes for medium-rare, turning once or twice. (If flare-ups occur, move the steak temporarily over indirect heat.) Transfer to a cutting board and let rest for 3 to 5 minutes.

Prepare the Charred Tomatoes and Onions

4. Grill tomatoes and onion halves over high heat until lightly charred. Allow to cool slightly, then coarsely chop. In a large bowl, toss tomatoes and onions with lime juice, oil, dill and chives. Season to taste with salt and pepper.

5. Cut steak against the grain into ½-inch (1 cm) slices. Fan slices out on a serving platter, top with Charred Tomatoes and Onions, sprinkle with blue cheese and garnish with chives.

Serves 4

1 flank steak (1½ to 2 pounds/675 to 900 g and about ¾ inch/2 cm thick)

Marinade
⅓ cup (75 mL) extra-virgin olive oil
4 sprigs thyme, leaves only
½ cup (125 mL) packed flat-leaf parsley leaves
½ cup (125 mL) packed cilantro
1 tablespoon (15 mL) Dijon mustard (I like Kozlik's Sweet and Smokey Mustard)
1 teaspoon (5 mL) kosher salt
1 teaspoon (5 mL) cracked black pepper

Charred Tomatoes and Onions
2 beefsteak tomatoes, cut into ½-inch (1 cm) rounds
1 medium red onion, halved through root end
Juice of 1 lime
2 tablespoons (30 mL) extra-virgin olive oil
1 tablespoon (15 mL) finely chopped dill
1 tablespoon (15 mL) finely chopped chives
Kosher salt and cracked black pepper

To Serve
½ cup (125 mL) crumbled blue cheese
Chopped chives

ZUCCHINI AND SUMMER SQUASH

Are you ready for summer's most prolific producers? This is one of the easiest vegetables to grow, and they can become giants in your garden! Zucchini, the best-known summer squash, is mild tasting and delicious in both savoury and sweet dishes. There are many other varieties of summer squash, all with their own textures, flavours and uses. This summer, explore your farmers' market and try a few new varieties, like crookneck, Zephyr, pattypan or tatuma squash. And we can't forget the blossom. These delicate flowers offer a gentle flavour and beautiful colour. They taste great stuffed and fried—I highly suggest trying a batch of my Tempura Zucchini Flowers with Lemony Ricotta—but are also wonderful gently torn and served over pasta or risotto or tossed with a salad.

This is one of my favourite zucchini side dishes. In this recipe, I fill zucchini with orzo, but you could use rice, couscous or quinoa instead. This easy-to-prepare summer dish is packed full of fresh flavours, and is a great choice for a light entrée on a warm summer night.

ZUCCHINI STUFFED with ORZO and CHEDDAR

1. Preheat oven to 375°F (190°C) and line a baking sheet with parchment paper.

2. Cook orzo according to package directions until al dente. Drain, transfer to a large bowl and toss with oil. Set aside.

3. Place raisins in a small bowl, cover with boiling water and let soak for 5 minutes to plump.

4. Drain raisins and add to orzo. Add sunflower seeds, pumpkin seeds, dill, parsley, chives and lemon zest and juice. Toss gently to combine. Season to taste with salt and pepper, then spoon mixture into zucchini halves.

5. Place stuffed zucchini on baking sheet. Bake until zucchini is fork-tender, 12 to 15 minutes. Set oven to broil, top zucchini with cheddar and Parmesan and broil until cheeses melt, about 5 minutes more. Serve immediately.

Serves 4

1 cup (250 mL) orzo
1 teaspoon (5 mL) canola oil
¼ cup (60 mL) seedless raisins
¼ cup (60 mL) toasted sunflower seeds
¼ cup (60 mL) toasted pumpkin seeds
1 tablespoon (15 mL) finely chopped dill
1 tablespoon (15 mL) finely chopped flat-leaf parsley
1 tablespoon (15 mL) finely chopped chives
Grated zest and juice of ½ lemon
Kosher salt and cracked black pepper
4 medium zucchini, halved lengthwise and seeded
½ cup (125 mL) grated white cheddar cheese
¼ cup (60 mL) finely grated Parmesan cheese

Squash blossoms, stuffed with creamy lemony ricotta, battered and fried are crunchy, salty and utterly addictive. Tempura zucchini flowers are a wonderful snack or appetizer. Or serve them up for brunch—your guests will flip out!

TEMPURA ZUCCHINI FLOWERS with LEMONY RICOTTA

Serves 4

¾ cup (175 mL) all-purpose flour

6 tablespoons (90 mL) cornstarch

1 teaspoon (5 mL) baking powder

1 teaspoon (5 mL) kosher salt, divided

1 cup (250 mL) sparkling water

1 cup (250 mL) smooth ricotta cheese

½ cup (125 mL) finely grated Parmesan cheese, plus more for garnish

Grated zest of ½ lemon

1 tablespoon (15 mL) lemon juice

3 basil leaves, thinly sliced into ribbons

1 teaspoon (5 mL) minced serrano chili

1 teaspoon (5 mL) cracked black pepper

8 very fresh zucchini flowers, stamen and pistil removed

Canola oil, for deep-frying

1. In a medium bowl, whisk together flour, cornstarch, baking powder, ½ teaspoon (2 mL) salt and sparkling water until smooth.

2. In another bowl, whisk together ricotta, ½ cup (125 mL) Parmesan, lemon zest, lemon juice, basil, chili, black pepper and remaining ½ teaspoon (2 mL) salt until smooth.

3. Spoon 1 heaping teaspoonful of ricotta mixture into centre of each zucchini flower and fold petals over to enclose filling. Do not overfill. Set aside.

4. In a medium, deep saucepan, heat 4 inches (10 cm) oil to 350°F (180°C).

5. Working in batches, dip zucchini flowers into batter, gently place in hot oil and fry until golden, about 5 minutes. Transfer zucchini flowers to paper towel to drain.

6. Arrange warm zucchini flowers on a serving platter, garnish with more grated Parmesan and serve immediately.

This is a great meal to make on those hot days when you don't want to have a heavy meal. The warm pork and a fresh, crisp noodle salad are a perfect summer pairing. This one will have you coming back for seconds!

BARBECUED PORK TENDERLOIN with SUMMER NOODLE SALAD

Make the Marinade and Prepare the Pork Tenderloin

1. In a small bowl, whisk together soy sauce, garlic, ginger, oil, mustard and sambal oelek until blended. Pour over pork, cover and refrigerate for at least 1 hour or overnight.

Make the Summer Noodle Salad

2. Place rice noodles in a large bowl, trying to snap as few of them as possible as you remove them from the package. Bring a good amount of water to a boil. Pour the boiling water over the rice noodles until they are submerged. Every minute or two, give the noodles a stir to loosen them up. When they are completely limp, test one to see if they're cooked through. Vermicelli noodles will cook through in just a few minutes, while flat rice noodles may take upwards of 10 minutes, depending on their thickness. Pay attention and test the noodles frequently, because they'll become mushy if they overcook. Once noodles are tender, drain and rinse under cold running water to stop the cooking process. Drain well again and transfer to a large bowl.

3. To make the dressing, in a small bowl, combine vinegar, soy sauce, coconut and sesame oils, lime juice, sugar, ginger, sambal oelek and pepper to taste. Whisk together well and adjust seasoning with more soy sauce and pepper if necessary. Dressing will keep refrigerated in an airtight container for up to 2 weeks.

4. To bowl of noodles, add zucchini, summer squash, cucumber, carrot and the dressing; gently toss until combined. Set aside in the refrigerator.

Barbecue the Pork Tenderloin

5. Prepare the grill for direct cooking over medium heat.

6. Remove pork from marinade and discard marinade. Grill pork over direct heat, with the lid closed as much as possible, until the outsides are evenly seared and the centre is barely pink, 15 to 20 minutes, turning every 5 minutes or so. The internal temperature should be 150°F (65°C). Remove from the grill, tent with foil and let rest for 3 to 5 minutes before slicing into ½-inch (1 cm) rounds.

7. Garnish Summer Noodle Salad with bean sprouts, peanuts, mint, cilantro and chives and serve alongside Barbecued Pork Tenderloin.

Serves 4

2 pork tenderloins (2 pounds/900 g total), trimmed

Marinade

¼ cup (60 mL) soy sauce
1 tablespoon (15 mL) minced garlic
1 tablespoon (15 mL) minced peeled fresh ginger
1 tablespoon (15 mL) olive oil
1 tablespoon (15 mL) Dijon mustard
2 teaspoons (10 mL) sambal oelek

Summer Noodle Salad

1 package (8 ounces/225 g) thin vermicelli rice noodles
¼ cup (60 mL) seasoned rice vinegar
¼ cup (60 mL) soy sauce
¼ cup (60 mL) coconut oil
1 tablespoon (15 mL) sesame oil
3 tablespoons (45 mL) lime juice
1 tablespoon (15 mL) dark brown sugar
2 teaspoons (10 mL) minced peeled fresh ginger
2 teaspoons (10 mL) sambal oelek
Cracked black pepper
1 small zucchini, seeded and julienned
1 small summer squash, seeded and julienned
1 English cucumber, seeded and julienned
1 small carrot, peeled and julienned

To Serve

Fresh bean sprouts
Chopped peanuts
Mint leaves, chopped
Cilantro leaves, chopped
Chopped chives

If you're like me and grow zucchini in your backyard, you know that when they start to come into season, you end up with a lot of zucchini. I'm pretty sure that zucchini bread is the reason zucchini exists, and this is my go-to recipe. It's perfect any time of day—for breakfast, brunch, teatime or dessert.

ZUCCHINI BREAD with WALNUT-HONEY BUTTER

Makes 1 loaf

Zucchini Bread

3 cups (750 mL) all-purpose flour
1 tablespoon (15 mL) cinnamon
1 teaspoon (5 mL) baking soda
1 teaspoon (5 mL) baking powder
1 teaspoon (5 mL) salt
3 large eggs
2¼ cups (550 mL) granulated sugar
1 cup (250 mL) vegetable oil
1 tablespoon (15 mL) pure vanilla
    extract
2 cups (500 mL) grated zucchini
1 cup (250 mL) chopped walnuts

Walnut-Honey Butter
Makes about 1 cup (250 mL)

1 cup (250 mL) unsalted butter, at
    room temperature
2 tablespoons (30 mL) honey
2 teaspoons (10 mL) grated orange
    zest
½ cup (125 mL) finely chopped
    toasted walnuts

Make the Zucchini Bread

1. Preheat oven to 350°F (180°C) and grease an 8- × 4-inch (20 × 10 cm) loaf pan.

2. In a medium bowl, stir together flour, cinnamon, baking soda, baking powder and salt until combined. In a large bowl, whisk together eggs, sugar, oil and vanilla until blended. Fold in zucchini and nuts until combined.

3. Add dry mixture to wet mixture and stir just until combined. Spoon batter into loaf pan and smooth the top.

4. Bake for 1 hour or until a toothpick inserted in centre of loaf comes out clean. Let cool in pan on a wire rack for 10 minutes, then turn loaf out onto rack and cool completely.

Make the Walnut-Honey Butter

5. In a small bowl, stir together butter, honey and orange zest until blended, then fold in walnuts. Butter can be stored in the refrigerator in an airtight container for up to 2 weeks.

6. Once cool, slice zucchini bread and serve with Walnut-Honey Butter.

ACKNOWLEDGEMENTS

Many thanks to all of these exceptionally talented, smart, funny, passionate, food-loving women who made this beautiful book with me! Lora Kirk, Sasha Seymour, Virginia McDonald, Debbie Rankine, Flo Leung, Alexandra Leggat, Rachel Brown and Andrea Magyar.

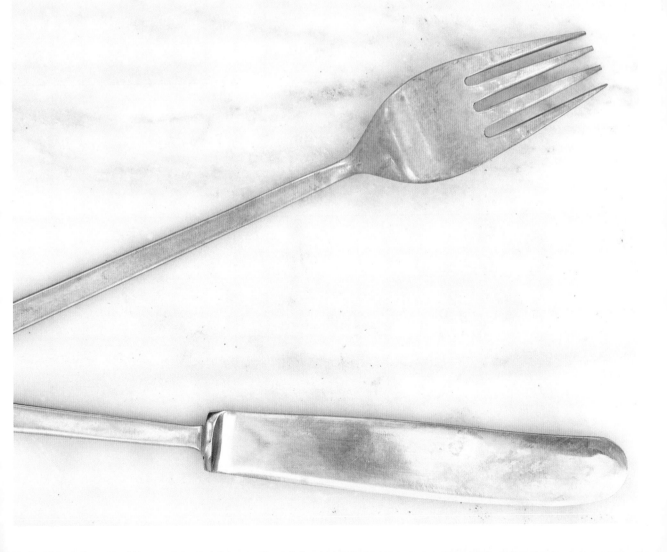

INDEX

Page numbers in bold indicate a discussion of the ingredient.